Explorers
of the
Pacific Northwest

Dedicated to Cy Groves and Margaret Frazer,

teachers who challenged us

Betty Sherwood and Janet Snider

canchron books
Canadian Chronicles
Toronto, Canada

Acknowledgements

We wish to thank the following people for their support and assistance during the creation of this book:
Jim Casquenette, Scott Bradford, Jean Shippey, Jacqueline Snider, Mary and Brick Bradford, Jim Barnum, Sandra Birnbaum, Laura Cairns, Marilyn Dodds, Paula Dotey, Joe Duerr, Daniel Desjardins, Donna Lightfoot, Elisabeth Lovell, Joan Martin, Christine Mueller, Marlene O'Brien (Bayfield Berry Farm), David Ridley, John Ridley, Dara Savarin Gold, Judith Walker, Chris Harris, Derek Hayes, Franco di Lieto, Staff of the Toronto Public Library

National Library of Canada Cataloguing in Publication

Sherwood, Betty, 1943-

Explorers of the Pacific Northwest / Betty Sherwood and Janet Snider.

(Explorer chronicles)

Includes bibliographical references and index.

ISBN 0-9688049-2-6

1. Explorers—Northwest, Pacific—Biography—Juvenile literature.

2. Northwest, Pacific—Discovery and exploration—Juvenile literature.

I. Snider, Janet, 1944- II. Title. III. Series.

FC3821.S53 2003   j979.5'02   C2003-904327-4

Print Production by Tibbles Bird & Company
Toronto, Canada

Contents

About the Quotations

The quotations taken from the various journals contain spelling, capitalization, terminology, and sentence structures that are not used today. We decided to use the accounts the way they were written to give the reader an appreciation of the writing customs of the period. Keep in mind that these journalists were not necessarily writers and these were their personal observations.

Introduction

The Pacific Northwest Coast of North America was visited by many explorers and traders before Captain Cook arrived in 1778. Two hundred years earlier in 1577, Sir Francis Drake, an English ship's captain and explorer, was commissioned by Queen Elizabeth I to sail to the Spanish colonies on the Pacific Coast of the New World. He plundered Spanish ports and captured Spanish ships along the way. He made use of their more

accurate maps to look for a passage through the continent to the east. He may have sailed as far north as today's Canada-U.S. border. He repaired his ship, the *Golden Hinde,* at Drake's Bay near present-day San Francisco, called the land New Albion and claimed it for Britain. He continued on his expedition and became the first Englishman to circumnavigate the world. He is most famous for leading the Royal Navy against the Spanish Armada and defeating it in 1587.

The Russians were also active on the Pacific Northwest Coast. In 1725 Czar Peter the Great ordered an expedition led by Vitus Bering to find out whether there was a passage between the Pacific and the Arctic Oceans. The Russians secured a foothold in Alaska where they explored and traded with the Natives.

The Spanish were already well established in California in 1774 when they sent the first expedition north commanded by Juan Perez. He was commissioned to explore along the Pacific Northwest Coast in order to protect Spanish sovereignty from the Russians who were setting up fur trading posts in Alaska.

The British, Spanish and Russians were all active along the Pacific Northwest Coast when Captain Cook arrived.

Captain James Cook

(1728 - 1779)

Captain James Cook

Captain James Cook has been described as perhaps the most important figure in the history of maritime exploration. His biographers seem puzzled by his excellent career and the many accomplishments by a man of such humble birth. James was born on October 27, 1728 in Yorkshire, England. His father was a hired farm labourer. James was "taught his letters" by Mrs. Walker, the wife of a freehold farmer. When James was eight, his father became the foreman of Anyholme Farm. Thomas Skotlowe who was a member of the gentry owned it.

When James was growing up, there was no free schooling for children. A small school had been established in a town close to the farm. Mr. Skotlowe recognized James's ability to learn and paid for his education. He was excellent at arithmetic. His later career shows that he was also curious and thorough.

While still a boy, it was clear that he was not a follower; he liked to decide his own way and then he followed his chosen path with determination and perseverance. He was obstinate, but must have also had a charming disposition because he was well liked. Throughout his life, people who could help him in his career guided him and taught him the skills he needed to achieve his goals.

He had several jobs before he went to sea. He worked on the farm during his teens, which developed his physical strength and endurance. At seventeen he became a shop clerk in Staithes, a fishing village. He had to live in the shop because it was too far to go home. He kept his bed and a few belongings under the shop counter. James worked there for eighteen months and then decided to go to sea. Mr. Sanderson, the shopkeeper, took

James to Whitby, a major shipbuilding town where they met John Walker, a Quaker ship owner. James Cook signed on as a bound apprentice for three years. That meant he would be a servant but also learn the trade of the sea.

Cook's first experience at sea was on a Whitby "cat", a collier that carried 500 tons of coal, had three masts with square-rigged sails and a flat bottom. Each year 400 ships transported coal from Newcastle to the market in London. During his apprenticeship he learned how important it was to the safety of the ship and to the rest of the crew that he be competent at his job.

Cook was promoted to Mate on Walker's ship and at 27 years old he was offered command of his own ship.

Whalebones in Whitby, England
with David Ridley (6 feet, 2 inches tall)

1729
Charles Perrault produced "Tales of Mother Goose".

1739
There were 551 coffee houses in London.

1739
Swedish astronomer Anders Celsius proposed the Celsius scale thermometer.

He decided to turn down the offer and instead he volunteered for service in the Royal Navy. A week after he joined the navy he was a sailor on the 60-gun warship, *Eagle*. One month later, he was promoted to Master's Mate. The Sailing Master was a position of great prestige and importance because the Master knew more than anyone else on the ship how to deal with the sails and rigging in order to get the vessel to its destination.

From 1754-1763, the Seven Years War was waged between Britain and France. This war brought James Cook to Canada. Prime Minister William Pitt realized that the greater battle was not in India or Europe but in North America. Because the British Navy was supreme, Pitt was successful in cutting the supply lines to New France. Cook arrived at Louisbourg in 1757 where the Royal Navy was attacking French warships. Cook was promoted to Master of the *Medway* after their victory over the French warship, *Duc d'Aquitaine*. Later he was made Master of the *Pembroke* under Captain John Simcoe, a famous captain who was the father of John Graves Simcoe, future Governor of Upper Canada. Simcoe encouraged Cook's continued scientific study so that he was able to accumulate the skills to make maps and charts. Cook was recognized as a serious mapmaker in 1759 after he produced a chart of the Gaspé Peninsula.

An Interesting Aside

The tents that Governor John Graves Simcoe and his family lived in during 1790 in Niagara-on-the-Lake were the same ones Captain Cook had carried around the world on his later voyages.

1742-1807
Joseph Brant (Thayendanega) was a Mohawk chief who became a colonel in the British Army.

1743
The first rules of boxing, drafted by John Broughton, were approved.

1748
The ruins of Pompeii were discovered.

In 1758, the military forces commanded by General Wolfe had orders to take Québec, but there were no reliable maps of the narrow waterway near the city. The ships could not sail close to their target safely. It was difficult to navigate the river near Québec, called the Traverse, because the tide fluctuated and the strong current made it difficult to move large ships with sails. This is where Cook used his skills to chart the St. Lawrence River so that eventually the ships could move into the south channel at Île d'Orléans. Montcalm, the French General, watched the laborious sounding and setting of buoys to mark the safe channel and was reported to have said, "Now there will be a good chart of the river."

The British ships were all close anchored when the French sent fireships loaded with hot shot (round iron balls heated to red-hot in furnaces) that was fired at the British ships to set them ablaze. The ships were all made of wood so fire was a dangerous hazard. The French had some success with the assault, but the British

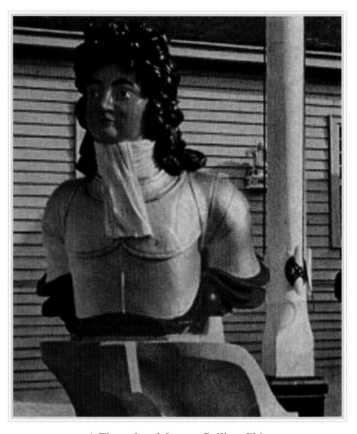

A Figurehead from a Sailing Ship

seamen were well-trained and able to avoid huge losses of ships and sailors. Montcalm commended the Royal Navy when he said, "It is quite probable that in similar conditions a French fleet would have perished."

On July 12, the British began to bombard Québec from Lévis with carcasses which were sod and paper cylinders containing burnable materials that were set alight when fired and burned long enough to set the wooden buildings in the city on fire. The inhabitants of Québec were under attack.

Wolfe knew that he had to take the city before the end of September or the troops would have to retreat to Nova Scotia for the winter. In order to gain time while he searched for a way up to the city, he moved his ships back and forth along the 24 km (15 miles) of shoreline above Québec. The French troops marched back and forth along the shore as the ships moved, in order to prevent the British troops from landing. By the time Wolfe actually made his assault on Québec, the French troops were exhausted.

Wolfe had found a cleft in the cliff that led up to the Plains of Abraham. Montcalm was expecting an attack from the other side of the city at Beaufort so Wolfe staged a false assault there while he moved most of his troops up the cliff. All night the troops climbed the steep cliff and amassed outside the city walls. When Montcalm got word that the British had scaled the cliff, he assembled his troops consisting of French regulars, Canadian colony troops and militia, and marched them to the Plains of Abraham. The end came swiftly. Wolfe died during the battle and Montcalm was mortally wounded and died later. The colony troops and militia fiercely defended Québec, but the French regulars turned and ran for the city gates. The battle took place on September 13, 1759 and surrender came five days later.

Captain James Cook
by Thomas Cook
after Lewis Pingo

After the battle at Québec, Cook went back to Nova Scotia and then returned to Britain in 1761. He married Elizabeth Batts in December 1762. In April 1763, he was commissioned to survey the coastline of Newfoundland and Labrador for the newly appointed governor. In the Treaty of Paris that ended the Seven Years War, France kept St. Pierre and Miquelon, two islands in the Gulf of St. Lawrence, to be used as bases for fishing. He had to chart these islands first because officials in Britain wanted to know exactly what was given to France. From 1763-1767 Cook charted the coasts of Newfoundland and Labrador. His charts were so accurate they were still being used 100 years later.

James Cook was promoted to captain and then from 1768-1778 Cook made three voyages to the Pacific Ocean. (see Cook's Voyages p. 16) On the third voyage he came to Canada as captain of the expedition to chart the West Coast of Canada from Vancouver Island to Alaska. On Sunday March 29, 1778 Cook wrote:

"…we no sooner drew near the inlet than we found the coast to be inhabited and the people came off to the Ships in Canoes without showing the least mark of fear or distrust. We had at one time thirty-two Canoes filled with people about us…they seemed to be mild unoffensive people, shewed great readiness to part with anything they had and took whatever was offered to them in exchange, but were more desirous of iron than any thing else…Monday 30th In the morning I sent three armed boats under the command of Mr. King to look for a harbour for the Ships and soon after I went myself in a small boat on the same service…I found a pretty snug Cove."

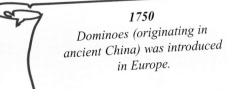

1750
Dominoes (originating in ancient China) was introduced in Europe.

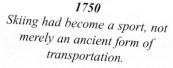

1750
Skiing had become a sport, not merely an ancient form of transportation.

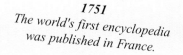

1751
The world's first encyclopedia was published in France.

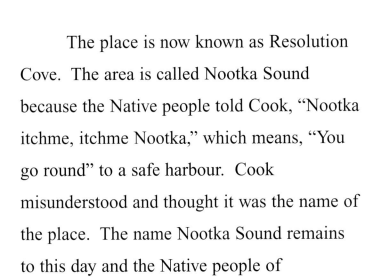

The place is now known as Resolution Cove. The area is called Nootka Sound because the Native people told Cook, "Nootka itchme, itchme Nootka," which means, "You go round" to a safe harbour. Cook misunderstood and thought it was the name of the place. The name Nootka Sound remains to this day and the Native people of Vancouver Island have adopted Nootka as their name.

Nootka Man in Hat

During their month-long stay, new masts were constructed and other repairs were made to the ship *Resolution*. Cook went out mapping as described by Midshipman Trevenen:

"...we rowed Cook not less than 30 miles during the day. We were fond of such excursions, although the labour of them was very great; as not only was this kind of duty more agreeable than the humdrum routine on board the ships, but as it gave us an opportunity of seeing different peoples and countries, and also another principal consideration, we were sure to have plenty to eat and drink...Captain Cook also on these occasions would sometimes relax from his almost constant severity of disposition and condescend now and then to converse familiarly with us. But it was only for a time; as soon as on board the ship he became again a despot."

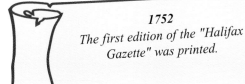

1752
The first edition of the "Halifax Gazette" was printed.

1755
The Acadians were expelled from Nova Scotia.

1755
An earthquake in Lisbon killed 15,000 people.

They also traded with the Native people, called the Mowachaht, for sea otter pelts. They developed a good trading relationship with them and were able to obtain many necessary supplies as well as a large number of otter pelts for trade in Russia.

On April 26, before Cook and his crew left, Chief Maquinna came aboard and presented Cook with a wonderful beaver skin cloak. In return, Cook gave the Chief a broad sword with a brass hilt.

The *Resolution* and *Discovery* left Nootka Sound to chart the waters of Alaska and search for a Northwest Passage through the Arctic. Cook was using Russian charts for this expedition, which were inaccurate and therefore unreliable. It took three months of mapping and talking to the local people along the Alaskan coast and the Aleutian Islands before the ships entered Bering Strait.

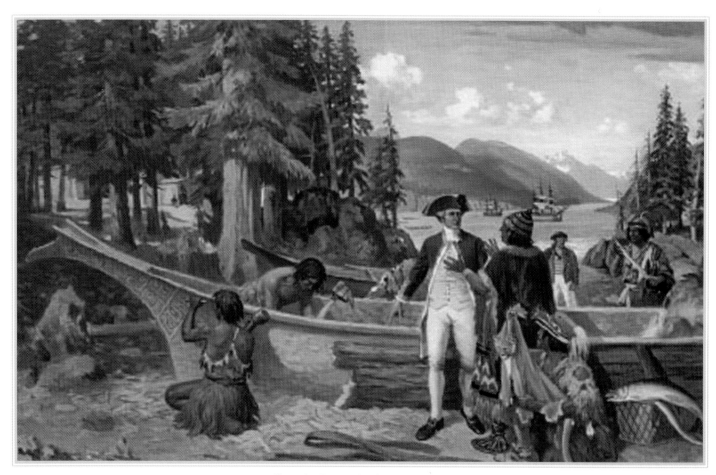

Captain James Cook by J. D. Kelly

The long voyage must have been wearing Cook down because sometimes his decisions were questionable. He continued to sail in fog while exploring the Aleutian Islands. When the crew heard waves breaking on rocks or a shore, Cook ordered, "Let go anchor". When the fog cleared, they looked back and saw that they had sailed through the only passage between two rock pinnacles. As Cook mopped his brow, he was heard to say, "I would not have tried that on a clear day." James King described the end of the quest for the Northwest Passage:

> "All our sanguine hopes begin to revive and we already begin to compute the distance of our situation from the known parts of Baffin Island. But after a few hours a strange white light was seen in the distance. As the ships approached it, a solid wall of ice was soon found to stretch from horizon to horizon. The ships fell into a gloomy routine of creeping through fog along an endless cliff face of ice. Guided only by the monotonous groaning of walruses on the edge of the ice floes."

The crew was relieved and happy when Cook announced they were going to sail to Hawaii.

Cook was killed in a skirmish with Hawaiian Natives soon after they arrived at Kealakekua Bay.

Sea Horses (Walruses)

Cook's Ships at Nootka

James Cook had such a fine reputation as a captain that to "have sailed with Cook" gave every seaman and officer great credentials for his future career. He insisted on individual competence regardless of social status, so all the men were highly skilled. He also had a good reputation with his crews because he kept them healthy. Scurvy was a dreaded disease that killed many sailors but not on Cook's ships. He insisted on good hygiene and that his men drink spruce beer, fruit juices and eat sauerkraut. Fresh provisions such as berries and vegetables were obtained as often as possible. He lost only one sailor to scurvy during all of his voyages.

1759-1796
Robert Burns was a Scottish poet whose poems and songs are loved worldwide.

1760
The first roller skates were worn at a masquerade in London.

1762
John, fourth Earl of Sandwich, invented a new dish: the sandwich.

Cook was a labourer who knew how to make rigging, yet he entered the world of gentlemen. The Royal Navy was the one area of endeavour where such a rise was possible due to the fact that merit and ability to learn to be a seaman, as well as the physical stamina necessary to survive on shipboard, were the qualities that were valued. Because Cook was so skilled, he was able to become a captain, a very high rank in the tightly structured and unfair British society of the 18th century. The Royal Society awarded him the Copely Gold Medal, Britain's highest honour for intellectual achievement.

Replica of the Endeavour

Cook's cottage was moved from Great Ayton in Yorkshire to Melbourne, Australia by Sir Russell Grimwade in 1933, as a gift to his fellow citizens.

1765
Québec City saw the first observance of St. Patrick's Day in Canada.

1769-1812
Sir Isaac Brock was a general and hero of the War of 1812.

1769
James Bruce discovered the source of the Blue Nile.

Voyages to the South Seas

In 1716 Edmund Halley, Astronomer Royal, predicted that Venus would cross in front of the sun on June 3, 1769, and that this event would not occur again until 1874. The Royal Society for Improving Knowledge was established in 1645. The members were wealthy and knowledgeable amateurs seeking scientific knowledge. The Royal Society wanted to sponsor, along with the King George III, a voyage to the South Pacific to observe the Transit of Venus. This was important because if the transit were recorded from several widely different positions on Earth, then the distance of the Sun from the Earth could be calculated. This distance, 155 million km (93 million miles), was unknown until 1769.

On August 26, 1768, Captain Cook led this expedition of 94 crew and 11 scientists. They were bound for Tahiti via the East Coast of South America and around Cape Horn. They met Natives in Tierra del Fuego and described them: "They are something above middle size of dark copper Colour with long black hair, they paint their bodies in Streaks mostly Red and Black, their clothing consists wholly of …seal. They didn't have any useful Utensils except it be a Bagg or Basket to gather Muscels into: in a word they were perhaps as miserable a set of people as are this day on Earth." That may have been the British view of these

Natives, but they had found ways to survive in a dreadful climate. The ship carried on through the Strait of Magellan and into the Pacific Ocean, finally arriving in Tahiti on April 11, 1769.

The Tahitians came out to the ship in their canoes and welcomed the crew with gifts of coconuts. The Natives wanted whatever the British owned. Cook said, "It was a hard matter to keep them out of the Ship as they clime like Munkeys, but it is still harder to keep them from Stealing every thing that came within their reach, in this they were…expert."

Cook went about the business of finding a place for his observatory while the scientists examined the flora and fauna. The third of June was a cloudless day, perfect for observing the Transit of Venus.

After completing this scientific study, Cook had orders to look for a southern continent. Because of the bitter cold and bad weather in September, he decided to turn north to New Zealand. Cook circumnavigated the north and south islands in a figure eight. His famous biographer, Beaglehole, said, "Never has a coastline been so well laid down by a first explorer."

Cook and his crew sailed to Australia and charted its East Coast. The future site of Sydney was called Port Jackson. On their travels they met Australian Aborigines who Cook described as, "About as tall as Europeans, of a very dark brown colour but

A View of Huahiene in Hawaii

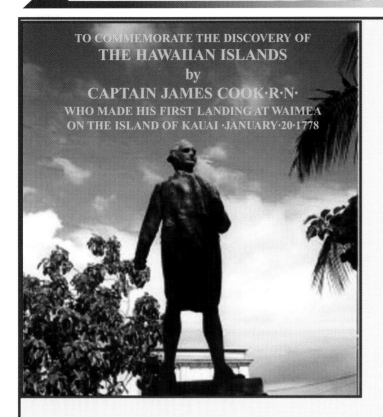

TO COMMEMORATE THE DISCOVERY OF
THE HAWAIIAN ISLANDS
by
CAPTAIN JAMES COOK·R·N·
WHO MADE HIS FIRST LANDING AT WAIMEA
ON THE ISLAND OF KAUAI ·JANUARY·20·1778

not black nor had they wooly frizled hair, but black and lank much like ours. No sort of clothing or ornaments were ever seen by any of us on them or about any of their hutts, from which I conclude that they never wear any. Some we saw had their bodies painted with a sort of white pigment."

On their voyage north, Cook had no way of knowing that they had entered a channel between the mainland and the Great Barrier Reef that got progressively narrower. Cook wrote in his journal: "A Reef such as is here…is scarcely known in Europe, it is a wall of Coral rock rising all most perpendicular out of the unfathomable ocean…the large waves of the vast Ocean meeting with so sudden a resistance make a most terrible surf breaking mountains high." The *Endeavour* hit the reef and took on water. Six cannon were thrown overboard to lighten the ship. The cannon remained on the reef for 200 years and were recovered in 1969, overgrown with coral but in good condition. Cook's flat-bottomed boat stayed upright and when the tide came in it lifted her off the reef so

that the other boats could tow her to land. The crew bandaged her with a sail around the damaged hull, much like a diaper, and floated her to the beach at the mouth of a river now called Endeavour. When the ship dried out, they found a great lump of coral still filling in the hole. This was why the ship didn't sink. They repaired the ship and then returned to Britain in 1771.

A year later, Cook again sailed to the South Pacific to search for a southern continent, as well as revisiting New Zealand and Tahiti. In 1776, Cook left Britain in the ships *Endeavour* and *Discovery* in command of the North Pacific expedition. He stopped in New Zealand and then went on to the Hawaiian Islands. From there Cook sailed to Nootka Sound on the West Coast of Canada. After completing the charting of the coast up to Alaska, the ships sailed back to Hawaii before returning to Britain. It was on this voyage that Cook died on Feb. 14, 1779. At Kealakekua Bay, there was a dispute over the theft of a boat. When Cook tried to settle the problem, he was set upon by Hawaiian warriors and killed along with four crewmen. Evidence suggests that the Hawaiians had come to regard Cook as the human form of their god, Lono. His ships were like floating islands and he gave them gifts. The former great chief, Lono, had promised to return on a floating island with trees and many gifts. Somehow Cook did not live up to their expectations and they turned on him. The expedition continued with John Gore, First Lieutenant, in charge and they returned to Britain in 1780.

Fifty years after Cook's death, a Maori chief paid tribute to him: "There was one supreme man in that ship. We knew he was the lord of the whole by his perfect gentlemanly and noble demeanor. He seldom spoke, but some of the 'goblins' spoke much. He came to us and patted our cheeks. This was the leader, which proved by his kindness to us, he is also very fond of children. A nobleman cannot be lost in the crowd."

The Nootka (Nun-Chah-Nulth)

Nun-Chah-Nulth means "those living at the foot of the mountains" and was officially adopted by the West Coast tribes as their name in 1978. The Mowachaht were a branch of the Northern Nootka living in the region when Cook arrived at Friendly Cove.

Lieutenant James King wrote about their first meeting: "We were surrounded by 30 or 40 canoes. It will require the assistance of one's imagination to have an adequate idea of the wild, savage appearance and actions of these first visitors...their dark copper-coloured bodies were so covered with filth as to make it a doubt what was really the proper colour; their faces were daubed with red and black paint and grease...to make themselves either fine or frightful."

Most of the descriptions of the Native people by Europeans only describe their appearance. Communication was difficult and often actions were misunderstood because they spoke different languages. Unless an explorer stayed for years, it was difficult to make accurate observations and to understand their customs and religion. There are few observations from the Native viewpoint but the following one, probably a story told for generations, describes Cook's arrival. Winifred David recorded this Mowachaht version in the 1970's. "The Indians didn't know what on earth it was when his ship came to the Harbour...so Chief Maquinna, he sent out his warriors...they went out to the ship and they thought it was a fish come alive in people. They were taking a good look at those white people on the deck there. One white man had a real hooked nose...he must have been a dog salmon. A man came out of the galley and he was a hunchback...these people must have been fish."

The Europeans would not have known that the Mowachaht religion included ceremonies apologizing to and thanking animals and fish for allowing them to be caught. Similarly, they would not know that the noise and wild actions were probably part of a ritual to welcome a visiting chief. Later, when fur traders arrived regularly, they became impatient with the length of the ceremony to welcome them before the trading could begin.

The Nootka were excellent woodworkers who made fine cedar canoes and built large houses that accommodated several families. They hunted and fished, and made the weapons and tools that they used. They made a whaling harpoon with a float and were the only West Coast tribe that hunted whale. This gave them economic advantages and prestige. The society was ranked from chief through commoners. They also had slaves who were the captives taken in wars. Property rights were closely guarded, including the rights to names, songs and stories. Chiefs were wealthy because they owned the most rights. The Mowachaht concern with property may explain the following

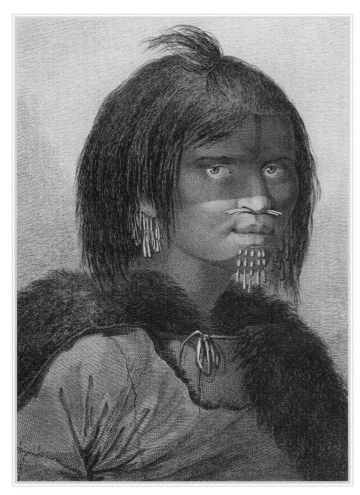

A Woman of Nootka

minutes, the man would demand another button. When Webber had no more brass buttons left, he was allowed to finish his drawing.

The Nootka presence on Vancouver Island dates back at least 4000 years. Trade and intermarriage occurred among the various bands of Nootka and with the Coast Salish that lived to the east and south. Trade with the European explorers was natural. Over the years the ships' crews brought diseases and alcohol that eventually reduced the Nootka population from 30,000 at first contact. In the 1800's they did not have sufficient population to oppose colonization or defend their rights. In the 1930's the population was about 2000. According to the 1996 census by Statistics Canada, there were 4,935 Nootka in British Columbia.

experience by Webber, the artist on Cook's ship, when he wanted to draw one of their houses. The gigantic house post decorated with carvings of animal figures impressed him. Shortly after he sat down to begin sketching, a young man of the house covered the post with a cedar mat and refused to allow Webber to continue until he had given him a brass button from his uniform. Every few

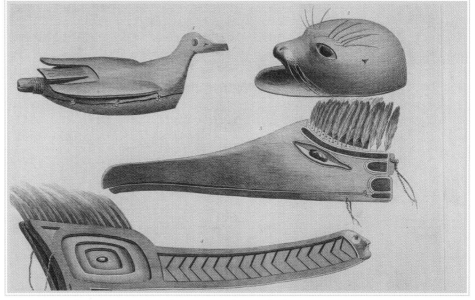

These Nootka masks and rattle were used at potlaches or feasts. The etching is based on a sketch by John Webber, 1778.

Captain George Vancouver

(1757-1798)

Captain George Vancouver
From a Painting by Lemuel F. Abbott

George Vancouver was born in King's Lynn, Norfolk on June 22, 1757. His father was a deputy collector of customs in this town on a bay called The Wash. His mother had six children with only one dying during childhood. George's parents, John Jasper and Bridget, had come from Couverden in Holland and took their surname from that town. Once in Britain, their name became Vancouver. George's older brother, John, says in his memoirs that George did well at King's Lynn Grammar School. When he was growing up, he read avidly. The travels of famous sailors were of great interest to him; Captain James Cook was his favourite and he dreamed of sailing with him. When George was 14, his father obtained a posting for him with Captain Cook on the *H.M.S. Resolution.* George's first voyage lasted four years from 1771 to 1775.

In August 1776 he sailed with Cook as a midshipman to the Pacific Northwest. While sailing with Cook, Vancouver learned navigation and map-making and became extremely proficient at both. On this voyage, Cook was killed in Hawaii in 1779. Captain Clerke took over command but died of tuberculosis, so Captain John Gore brought the ships back to Britian.

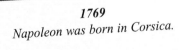

1769
Napoleon was born in Corsica.

1770-1827
Ludwig von Beethoven was the composer of some of the world's greatest music.

1772
Nitrous oxide (laughing gas) was discovered by Joseph Priestley.

George was promoted to lieutenant on his return in 1780. He was 23 years of age. Between 1785 and 1789, Vancouver sailed in the Caribbean Sea where he contracted several diseases that damaged his health for the rest of his life. In 1790, a fur trader named John Meares arrived in Britain with news that the Spanish had seized three of his ships at Nootka Sound. This incident was considered a threat to Britain by Spain. The British

Parliament was furious with the Spanish for assisting the Americans in their revolution against Britain. France, a usual ally of Spain, was embroiled in its own revolution, so when Britain mobilized the Royal Navy against Spain, the Spanish gave in at the threat of war. The Nootka Convention was the result. In this agreement, the Pacific Northwest was transferred from Spain to Britain.

On December 15, 1790, George Vancouver, now a captain at 33 years of age, led the *Discovery* and the *Chatham* on a voyage to the Pacific Northwest. He had orders to ratify the Nootka Convention when he arrived at Nootka Sound and to survey the northwest coast of America between the lands held by Spain and those held by Russia.

Statue of Vancouver Atop the B.C. Legislature

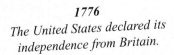

1776
The United States declared its independence from Britain.

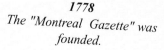

1778
The "Montreal Gazette" was founded.

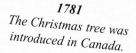

1781
The Christmas tree was introduced in Canada.

The ships travelled south along the coast of Africa. When they arrived in Tenerife, Canary Islands, Vancouver, as was the custom, paid his respects to the Spanish governor. Later, he and some of his officers dressed in civilian clothes and had dinner with some friends who lived there. While they were dining, a fight broke out amongst Vancouver's crew, and when the Spanish sentinel on duty attempted to break up the fight, he was attacked and the conflict escalated between the British sailors and the Spanish guards. Vancouver and his officers intervened, but because they were not in uniform, they were assaulted also. Vancouver was thrown into the sea and Lieutenant Baker was struck on the head with a musket. All survived, but it was a nasty incident. Captain Vancouver and the Spanish governor exchanged letters and admitted that there were errors on both sides; then the incident was forgotten.

This experience may have set the tone for the voyage because it was a difficult one where discipline was concerned. Vancouver was worried about the number of young aristocrats under his command because Captain William Bligh had returned to Britain in the previous year with eighteen loyal crew members in a seven metre (23 foot) launch that he had sailed 6000 km (3600 miles) from Timor in the Pacific Ocean. He reported that some of his crew, led by Fletcher Christian, an aristocrat, had mutinied on the *Bounty* near Tahiti. Vancouver had fifteen young gentlemen on his ships. There were 100 crew on the *Discovery*, which was 31 m. (99 feet) long and four storeys high. The *Chatham* had a crew of 53 and was 16 m. (53 feet) long. Archibald Menzies, the ship's doctor and botanist, added to the congestion by building a greenhouse that measured 2.5 m. by 3.7 m. (8 ft. by 12ft.) on the deck. The crowded conditions and the class differences made discipline hard to maintain.

Albatross

Vancouver applied punishment that he was entitled to administer, with regularity and according to the regulations of the Royal Navy. His officers gave him the respect he deserved as their captain, but there was little or no warmth towards him. The young gentlemen disliked and feared him. The ships were too small, which probably added to the discord.

When they arrived at the Cape of Good Hope on the southern tip of Africa, four men had to be sent home because the rigours of life on the ship were too great. Many of the crew were suffering from dysentery, so departure was delayed until they recovered.

A year after leaving Britain, the *Discovery* arrived at Matavia Bay, Tahiti.

The *Chatham* had arrived earlier. Broughton, Master of the *Chatham*, wrote, "Being informed by some of the natives that a ship was in sight, I repaired instantly to the shore and had the unspeakable pleasure of perceiving it to be the *Discovery* to the eastward, steering for the bay." Broughton's comments show how much he looked forward to seeing his comrades again when they reached port.

Until 1794, Vancouver's expedition charted the coast from California to Cook Inlet, Alaska. They spent the winters in Tahiti and returned in the spring to complete the survey.

Dysentery

This disease plagued sailors in the 18th century. The symptoms are diarrhea and severe stomach cramps. Dehydration of the patient is likely if fluids are not replaced. It is caused by amoebae or bacteria that infect water and food and thrive in unsanitary conditions.

Part of mapping the coast involved identifying and naming islands, mountains and bodies of water. Captain Vancouver named Mount Baker after Lieutenant Joseph Baker, Puget Sound after Lt. Peter Puget, Johnstone Strait after James Johnstone, Master of the *Chatham* and Mount Ranier after Admiral Peter Ranier, a friend in the Royal Navy. The majority of the surveying was done from open boats rowed along the coasts of the mainland and the islands that now belonged to the British Empire.

While the survey teams were out, there was much to be done on the moored ships. The carpenters repaired any leaks while the crew repaired the rigging, stored provisions and cleared the holds for shingle ballast used to stabilize the ships during sailing.

On shore, the sail makers repaired and altered the sails as necessary; coopers inspected the casks; gunners aired the gunpowder; sailors cut wood, brewed spruce beer and filled kegs with fresh water.

Vancouver and his crew were the first Europeans to see the area that is now the city of Vancouver. Near the mouth of the Capilano River, they met fifteen Natives in canoes near the present site of the Lions Gate Bridge. The ships continued eastward into Burrard Inlet as far as the present position of Port Moody, where the Canadian Pacific

Burrard Inlet, Vancouver, B.C.

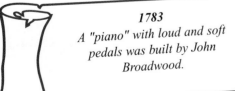

1783
A "piano" with loud and soft pedals was built by John Broadwood.

1783
The first balloons were constructed and flown by the Montgolfier brothers.

1783-1830
Simon Bolivar was a leader in the South American struggle for independence.

Captain George Vancouver by J.D. Kelly

Railway arrived in 1885. Vancouver relates an amusing incident:

" The shores of this situation were formed by steep rocky cliffs, that afforded no convenient place for pitching our tents, which compelled us to sleep in our boats. Some of the young gentlemen, however preferring the stony beach for their couch, without duly considering the line of high water mark, found themselves incommoded by the flood tide, of which they were not apprized until they were nearly afloat: and one of them slept so sound, that I believe he may have been conveyed some distance, had he not been awakened by his companions."

On June 22, 1792, the day Vancouver turned 35 years of age, he wrote:

" As we were rowing… for Point Grey, purposing there to land and have breakfast, we discovered two vessels at anchor…they were a brig and a schooner bearing the colours of Spanish vessels of war, which I conceived were most probably employed in a pursuit similar to our own…"

The Spanish commanders were Senor Don Galiano and Senor Don Valdes. They told Vancouver that Senor Quadra was waiting for him at Nootka Sound to arrange for the restoration of the territories to Great Britain. They were invited to have their breakfast on the Spanish ship.

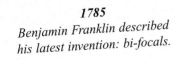

1785
Benjamin Franklin described his latest invention: bi-focals.

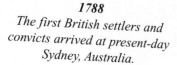

1788
The first British settlers and convicts arrived at present-day Sydney, Australia.

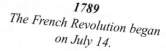

1789
The French Revolution began on July 14.

During their surveying trip between Vancouver Island and the mainland, there were many events recorded by Vancouver and his officers. Vancouver tells of a misunderstanding at a dinner attended by twelve Natives:

Galiano Island

"One part (of the dinner) was a venison pasty. Two of them, expressing a desire to pass the line of separation drawn between us, were permitted to do so. They sat down by us, and ate the bread and fish that we gave them without hesitation, but on being offered the venison, though they saw us eat it with great relish, they could not be induced to taste it. Their conduct on this occasion left no doubt in our minds that they believed it to be human flesh…and threw it down in the dirt with gestures of great aversion and displeasure. At length we happily convinced them of their mistake by showing them the haunch (of deer) in the boat.   Some of them ate the remainder of the pye with good appetite."

Puget describes the first recorded encounter of a skunk by Europeans:

"An animal called a skunk was run down by one of the Marines after Dark and the terrible stench it created absolutely awakened us in the tent. The smell is too bad for Description. This Man's Cloaths were afterwards so offensive that notwithstanding boiling they still retained the Stench of the Animal and in the next expedition others (clothes) were given him on Condition that those that retained the Smell should be thrown away and happy he was to comply with it."

Burrard Inlet Viewed from Spanish Banks

us company in our lonely searches, visited not these dreary shores." The Captain stopped the explorations and sailed for Nootka.

Senor Don Juan Francisco de la Bodegay Quadra was born in Lima, Peru in 1740. He had a charming personality and was a man of outstanding character and ability. He and Vancouver became friends immediately. Quadra had a farm at Nootka and provided food for the British sailors. His generosity must have been welcomed after their arduous journey of the last six months.

Lighthouse at Atkinson Point

Vancouver says he named Atkinson Point after a "particular friend", who may have been Edmund Atkinson, a master's mate, or Thomas Atkinson, a naval officer. The Point has become famous for its radio beacon and lighthouse flashing at the entrance to Vancouver harbour.

Because of the tides, undertow and foggy weather, both ships had run aground during the voyage around the Island. In his journal, Vancouver describes his experience of the country as, "…desolate and inhospitable a country as the most melancholy creature could be desirous of inhabiting. The eagle, crow and raven, that occasionally had borne

Plaque on Marine Drive, Vancouver, B.C.

***REUNION DE LOS CAPITANES BODEGA-QUADRA &
VANCOUVER***
Agosto de 1792
NOOTKA CONVENTION CONFERENCE
Donated by the Government of Spain 1957

Quadra and Vancouver were not bilingual. Luckily, Captain Dobson of the *Daedalus* was able to act as translator. After the business was finished and the lands had been transferred, Quadra suggested that they visit Maquinna, Chief of the Nootka, to show their respect. The dinner was memorable, with food provided by Quadra and "drinkables" by Vancouver. Mr. Bell described the entertainment in his journal: "Maquinna, dancing, now entered, dressed in a very rich garment of Otter skins with a round Black Hat, and a Mask on, with a fanciful petticoat or apron, around which was suspended hollow tubes of Copper and Brass and which as he danced, by striking against each other made a wonderful tingling noise."

Captain Quadra

After Maquinna and the other performers were finished their songs, the British sailors danced reels accompanied by a fife. They all left the Nootka village very late that evening. Vancouver sailed for Hawaii on October twelfth.

1791
Composer W.A. Mozart died at age 35.

1791
The metric system was introduced and adopted by law in France.

1797
The first recorded parachute jump was made by André-Jacques Garnerin in Paris.

Captain Vancouver's ships left Hawaii for the Pacific Northwest at the end of March 1793. On May 31, they were mapping near the mouth of the Bella Coola River north of Vancouver Island. Two months later, Alexander Mackenzie arrived at the Pacific Ocean via the Bella Coola River after having travelled overland across Canada.

Mapping the many islands and inlets along the North Pacific coast was very arduous. A large part of the work had to be done from small, open boats and the weather was cold with a lot of ice in the water. The large ships ran aground constantly in the uncharted waterways, adding to the difficulties for the crew. Ice broke the ships' mooring cables when the tides forced the ice back and forth against the cables.

By mid-July 1774, Vancouver's health was deteriorating so that he could not go out on excursions. From his fleshy appearance and protuberant eyes, it is believed that he had a thyroid condition. His cough seemed to rattle the whole ship.

Sailors Poisoned by Red Tide

Master Johnstone's mapping crew collected mussels, cooked and ate them. Several of the men felt numbness around their mouths and in their hands and feet. One sailor was so seriously affected that he couldn't breathe and later died. Carter's Bay bears his name and they called the channel Poison Cove. This paralytic shellfish poisoning is caused by a protozoan species that is eaten by mussels. These protozoa secrete a toxin that paralyzes muscle tissue in humans and other vertebrates. The organisms are red and change the colour of the water. It is called red tide.

1798
Alois Senefelder invented lithography as a cheap way of printing his plays.

1798
Edward Jenner publicized his successful smallpox vaccine.

1801
The Jacquard loom was the forerunner of the computer.

Some of his officers thought he might be suffering from temporary insanity because he lost his temper frequently. His officers and men respected him because of his position and his skill as a mapmaker and navigator, but no affection was directed towards him. The atmosphere was stiff and business-like on the crowded ships.

Although Vancouver was impatient with his men and lacked charm and humour, he had endless patience when engaged in astronomy and navigation. His expertise was impressive. He had learned to calculate longitude using lunar distances aboard the *Resolution* with Captain Cook. He calculated longitude correctly to within half a kilometre,

235° west of Greenwich, more than halfway around the Earth. Given the landforms, the sea and his health, this was brilliant.

The *Discovery* and the *Chatham* returned to Britain in 1795 after having been away from home for four years. Vancouver and his men had accomplished their tasks of mapping the Pacific Northwest Coast and accepting the transfer of Spanish land holdings to Great Britain. Vancouver retired with a naval pension but died two years later at only forty years of age.

A Man of Kamtschatka, Travelling in Winter by Webber, the Expedition Artist
Vancouver and his crew visited Russia on their way home.

DID YOU KNOW?

Sea Otters

The Canadian comeback-of-the year award for 2002 should go to the sea otter. A century ago sea otters were victims of the fur trade and they were hunted to extinction on the West Coast of Canada and the United States. Some sea otters survived in Alaska. Hunting was banned and then the population increased and started to move south. In 2002 these playful animals reached as far south as Tofino on Vancouver Island.

What's in a Name?

The fictional English Detective Chief Inspector Morse, who is famous for not revealing his first name, finally told a friend that his parents named him Endeavour because they admired Captain James Cook.

Places Named After Explorers

Cook Inlet is in Alaska.

Mount Vancouver, 4828 m. high, is near the Alaska-Yukon border.

Mackenzie Point, named by explorer John Franklin, is near the mouth of the Coppermine River.

The Fraser River was named by explorer David Thompson in honour of Simon Fraser.

Frances Barkley (1769-1845) sailed with her husband Captain Charles Barkley aboard the Imperial Eagle when she was 17. She is the first woman known to have circumnavigated the world. She was the first European woman to reach British Columbia during their voyage (1786-1788) to Nootka to trade for sea otter furs.

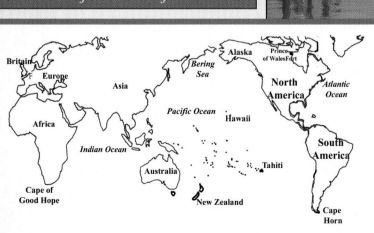

Transit of Venus

On August 10, 1768 two scientists, William Wales and Joseph Dymond, arrived at Prince of Wales Fort on the Churchill River. They stayed through the winter in order to observe the Transit of Venus on June 3, 1769. On the other side of the world in Tahiti, Captain James Cook was doing the same.

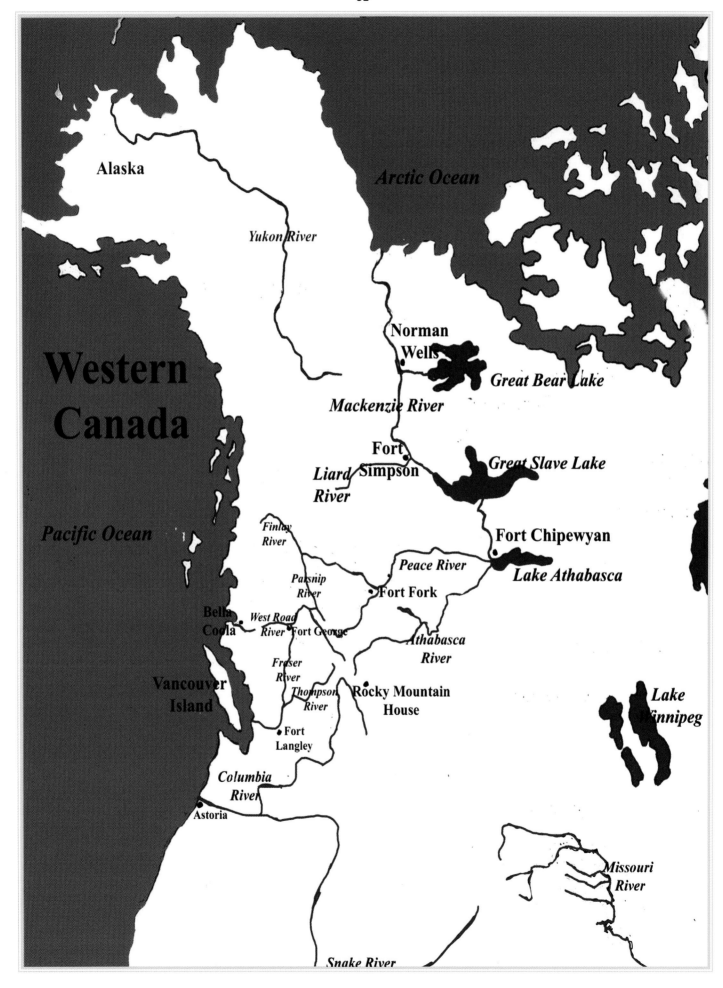

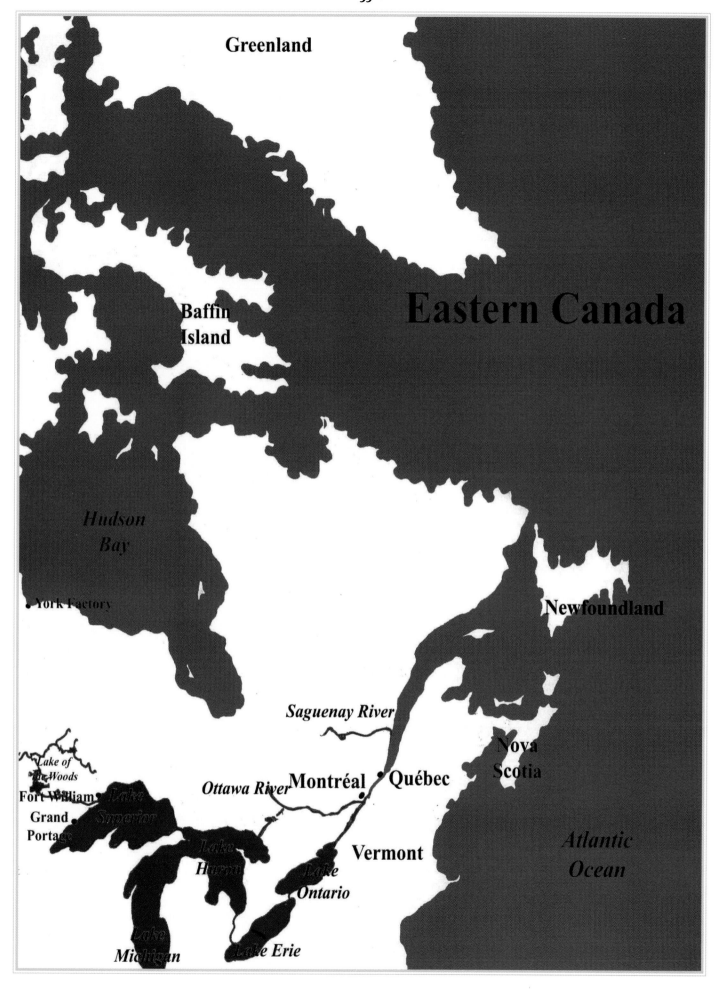

➤ DID YOU KNOW? ◀

"Canada's early explorers had to be pretty tough to survive the ordeals of surveying uncharted territories. In honour of these hardy men, Agriculture Canada created a series of equally tough roses," said Lois Hole. There are roses named Alexander Mackenzie, George Vancouver and Simon Fraser.

Origin of the Name Fraser

Fraser, a Norman family name, comes from the French word fraise meaning strawberry. The first Frasers arrived in Britain with William the Conqueror in 1066. Their coat of arms included the strawberry flower.

Fort Langley was a palisaded Hudson's Bay Company fort built in 1841 on the Fraser River, then abandoned in 1886. Now it is a National Historic Site. The only original building is the storehouse (building with shutters) where furs and goods similar to those traded and sold in the 1850's are displayed.

58° north is the latitude of Stornoway where Alexander Mackenzie was born. It is nearly the same latitude as Fort Chipewyan on Lake Athabasca.

Golden Hinde, at 2200 m., is the highest mountain on Vancouver Island. A full-scale reproduction of Sir Francis Drake's ship, the Golden Hinde, is on display near London Bridge in London, England.

In Canada one can travel from Montréal to the Pacific Ocean by canoe with the longest portage being 22 km (13 miles).

The City of Vancouver was incorporated on April 6, 1886. Native people have inhabited the area since at least 500 BC.

Sir Alexander Mackenzie
(1763-1820)

Sir Alexander Mackenzie was born in Stornoway, on the Isle of Lewis in Scotland. Growing up near the sea on the family farm, he probably had knowledge of boats and sailing from a young age. It is likely that he spoke Gaelic as well as English. In 1774, after his mother died, Alexander and his father, Kenneth, moved to New York to live with two of Alexander's aunts. When the American Revolutionary War started, Kenneth and his brother joined the British army. Alexander's aunts sent him to school in Montréal because they knew he would be safe there. After completing his schooling at 16 years of age, he started to work for a fur trading company. One of his biographers stated, "His keenness and daring at once attracted the attention of his employers, and his selection, after a very short experience, to

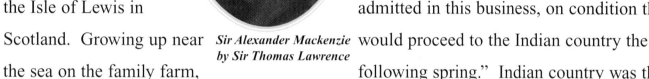

Sir Alexander Mackenzie by Sir Thomas Lawrence

lead a trading expedition to Detroit, on the lower lakes, was a remarkable example of confidence." At the age of 22, he was offered a partnership in the Gregory, MacLeod Company. Mackenzie writes, "Without any solicitation on my part, I had procured an insertion in the agreement that I should be admitted in this business, on condition that I would proceed to the Indian country the following spring." Indian country was the Canadian Northwest.

In 1783, the North West Company was formed and led the way in opening the west. Mackenzie was sent to the Churchill River Department at Île-à-la Crosse, [central Saskatchewan]. Mackenzie was moved to the North Country in 1788 to help Peter Pond at the Athabasca fur trading post. Pond knew the northern geography and the western flowing rivers had captured his imagination. His stories, told through the long winter, inspired Mackenzie's two historic voyages. Arthur Morton, a Canadian historian, says, "Mackenzie took the torch from Peter Pond's hand and pressed on with masterfulness, self control, in judgement all his own."

The Mackenzie River Expedition

Mackenzie wanted to find a river route to the Pacific Ocean. His company supported his plan because it would open more fur trading territory. Mackenzie set out from Fort Chipewyan on June 3, 1789 with a party of 14 people. They included Laurent Leroux, a trader, voyageurs Joseph Landry, Charles Ducette, François Barrieau, and Pierre de Lorme, three Native wives, Johann Steinbruck, and the Chipewyan Chief Nestabeck, also known as English Chief, and his two wives. Two young Natives travelled in a smaller canoe and they were hired as interpreters and hunters. Mackenzie's cousin Roderic, newly arrived from Scotland, stayed behind to 'hold the fort' while the others explored.

On the third day, they encountered a series of rapids on the Slave River near present-day Fort Smith. When they reached Great Slave Lake, it was still frozen. It took them three weeks to paddle across the lake and find the Mackenzie River. Laurent Leroux stayed at Great Slave Lake to gather furs while the rest of the party headed north. By July 1, they had reached the Liard River where Fort Simpson is located today. Throughout the trip, they had to put up with cold temperatures and swarms of mosquitoes.

They met members of the Slave and Dogrib tribes who were described by Mackenzie:

> **"They are of Medium Stature and as far as could be discerned through Dust and Grease that covered their whole Body fairer than the generality of Indians, who inhabit warmer climes… their ornaments consist of Bracelets, Gorgets (necklaces), Arm and Wrist Bands made of Wood, Horn or Bone; Belts, Garters and a kind of Cap which they wear on their Head made of a Piece of Leather 1 1/2 Ins. Wide embroidered with Porcupine Quills and stuck round with Claws of Bears or wild Fowls inverted to each of which hangs a few parings of fine white Ferret Skins in fashion as with a Tassel."**

Even though the river was not flowing west towards the Pacific Ocean and the Natives said it was a very long way to the ocean, Mackenzie wanted to continue.

Walrus

43 CANADA

Mackenzie River
Fleuve Mackenzie

Mackenzie wrote, "I sat up last Night to observe what time the Sun would set, but found that it did not set at all!" In the Mackenzie River delta they saw the remains of Inuit campsites but no Natives. They found two big skulls that they guessed were "sea horses" (walrus). They reached an island in the Arctic Ocean which he called Whale Island [Garry Island]. They stayed 3 1/2 days and saw pack ice all around which glowed white in the distance.

Mackenzie left a plaque reading:

> **69º14' Alexander Mackenzie**
> **and 5 men**
> **July 14, 1789**

He wasn't sure he had reached the Arctic Ocean because he didn't have the instruments to calculate longitude. He thought the tides were caused by the wind, and if he tasted the water, it would have been fresh because of the huge volume of water flowing from the Mackenzie River.

On their way back to Fort Chipewyan, they were paddling upriver against a very strong current. Often they had to tow their canoes with a rope while they walked along the shore. At Fort Norman, Mackenzie said, "The whole Bank was on fire for a considerable Distance." These coal seams were burning in 1789 and later in 1826 they were mentioned by John Franklin. They are still burning today. They reached Great Slave Lake after 8 days of towing, sailing and paddling their canoes. They met up with Leroux, who had been trading all summer. He was staying for the winter so Mackenzie handed over all his trading goods for Leroux to use. After saying farewell to the English Chief and his hunters, Mackenzie and the rest of the party set off. It took them 9 more days to reach Lake Athabasca. On September 12 Mackenzie wrote, "Froze hard last Night, Cold Weather throughout the Day, appearance of snow." The trip had taken 102 days and

Fort Chipeywan

the summer was over by the time they returned to Fort Chipewyan.

Mackenzie wintered at Fort Chipewyan, then paddled more than a month to reach Grand Portage on Lake Superior for the North West Company Partners meeting in July. He was awarded another share in the company, which gave him 10 percent of the shares. The partners were not impressed with his recent trip to the Arctic Ocean and neither was Mackenzie. He was disturbed by the fact that he could not determine his location exactly because he did not know how to calculate longitude. He decided to spend the winter in Britain studying astronomy and navigation and buying the instruments he needed.

1806
"Twinkle, Twinkle Little Star" was published by Ann and Jane Taylor.

1811
At age 11 Mary Anning found the first complete skeleton of an ichthyosaur.

1811
John McIntosh discovered an apple tree on his farm near Dundela, Upper Canada.

Mackenzie's Route to the Arctic Ocean
(from a Grade 7 project by JME)

He had a chronometer and had learned how to use it so now he could fix his location accurately. When he checked the position of Fort Chipewyan, he found that he was further east than he and Peter Pond had calculated. Now he knew that the distance to the Pacific Ocean was 1500 km (950 miles).

In planning his expedition to the Pacific Ocean, Mackenzie decided to set up a new fort, Fort Fork, on the Peace River, south of Fort Chipewyan. In his journal, he had noted that in 1788 a garden had been sown at this location, that had yielded a good crop of turnips, potatoes and cabbages. He wrote, "There is not the least doubt but the soil would be very productive if proper attention was given to the preparation." Mackenzie recognized the potential of this area of the Peace River, which is now an important agricultural region.

He travelled by canoe across Lake Huron, through Georgian Bay, along the French River, to the Ottawa River and then south to Montréal. This was the route that Champlain had taken to get to Huronia in 1615.

In the spring of 1792, Mackenzie sailed back to Montréal from Britain. After getting his supplies together, he retraced his route across Canada by canoe to Fort Chipewyan.

1814-1894
Adolphe Sax was the inventor of the saxophone.

1816
French physician René Laennec invented the stethoscope.

1816
Winter winds and snow struck Canada in June, July and August.

The Expedition to the Pacific Ocean

Mackenzie and the Voyageurs at the Pacific Ocean by C.W. Jefferys

Mackenzie was accompanied by six voyageurs: Joseph Landry, Charles Ducette, François Courtois, Baptist Bisson, Jacques Beauchamp, François Beaulieux and Alex Mackay, his second-in-command. The rest of the party included two Beaver Natives hired as hunters and interpreters and Mackenzie's dog. They built a canoe especially for the trip. The interior was 8m. (25 ft.) long and 1.5 m. (5 ft.) wide. When loaded, it weighed 1500 kg (3000 lb.) and sprang leaks the day after they left Fort Fork. They believed that it was bad luck to leave on a Friday, so they left on Thursday afternoon, May 9, 1793.

The Peace River was just freezing over when Mackenzie arrived at Fort Fork. He had sent a crew on ahead to start construction work. No buildings had been erected but the timbers were squared. He outfitted the Natives for winter hunting and trapping and then started building the fort. It consisted of a house, storehouses and palisades. During the winter, Mackenzie met and talked with Natives who told him that there was another great river towards the mid-day sun, whose current ran in that direction.

Peter Pond

Peter Pond was born in Connecticut in 1740. At 16 years of age he joined the British Army to fight against the French in New France. Then he entered the fur trading business and traded along the Mississippi River. In 1775 he went to the Canadian Northwest for the first time and traded along the Saskatchewan River. He had a flair for trading and developed a reputation for his ability to collect furs quickly. When he was based at Île-à-la Crosse, he followed the Native route west to Lac La Loche and found Athabasca Country when he portaged 22 km (13 miles) to the Clearwater River.

This became the famous portage called Portage La Loche or Methye Portage. He had crossed the Continental Divide that separated the rivers flowing north from those flowing south.

Pond also had a reputation for violence. In 1787, he or one of his men shot John Ross, a trader from a rival company. Ross was wounded and bled to death. This incident prompted several fur trading companies to merge with the North West Company to eliminate the competition that sometimes became deadly. In 1788 the North West Company wanted to fire Pond but not until he had passed on his knowledge of Athabasca Country to Alexander Mackenzie. Pond's information about the geography of the Northwest inspired both of Mackenzie's expeditions.

The Natives told Mackenzie that there were rapids through the Peace River Canyon. Mackenzie wrote, "In a distance of 2 miles we were obliged to unload 4 times and carry everything but the canoe." When the river became, "a white sheet of foaming water", they had to portage for 13 km (9 mi.). While in camp on May 30, the dog ran back and forth barking which warned the men of a wolf nearby. The next day they paddled to where the Peace River meets the Finlay and Parsnip Rivers. Following the advice of the Natives, they took the Parsnip River south.

They passed the present site of Mackenzie, British Columbia, and then the current became so strong that they couldn't paddle against it. The men pulled the canoe along using overhanging branches. When they camped, they found wild parsnips, for which the river was named, and boiled them to eat with their pemmican. A Sekani Native met them and told Mackenzie that he knew of a large river that ran toward the mid-day sun. He asked the man to draw a map and then by offering gifts, persuaded him to guide them. They paddled the length of Arctic Lake and

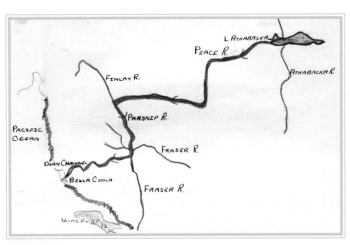

Mackenzie's Route to the Pacific Ocean
(from a Grade 7 project by JME)

then portaged to Portage Lake, Pacific Lake and then to James Creek. They had crossed the Continental Divide, so now they were travelling with the current to the West Coast.

Because it was spring, all the water levels were high and travelling was dangerous because of rapids and fallen trees. They had to travel this early in the year to get back to Fort Fork before autumn. The canoe was badly damaged when they were shooting the rapids. Mackenzie described, "This alarming scene with its terrors and dangers, occupied only a few minutes. When they (the Natives) saw our deplorable situation…(they) sat down and gave vent to their tears." All the men and the dog were safe but they had lost their ammunition. Most of the men wanted to go back, but Mackenzie used his considerable leadership ability to persuade them to go on. An extra measure of rum may also have helped push their fears into the background.

It took several days to repair the canoe, dry their gear and gunpowder and make more bullets. It took them five days to go 14 km (9 mi.). Mackenzie wrote, "The labour and fatigue of this undertaking beggars all description." The Sekani guide deserted but Mackenzie wrote, "At length we enjoyed, after all our toil and anxiety, the inexpressible satisfaction of finding ourselves on the banks of a navigable river on the West side of the first great range of Mountains." They had reached Herrick Creek. They stopped here for three days to build a new canoe.

On the West Road River, they met Carrier Natives who agreed to guide them on an overland route to the sea. They cached their canoe and supplies for the return journey and then followed the "grease trail". This was an overland route used to carry eulachon oil that came from a smelt-like fish. It was used by the Carrier to tan and protect moose, deer and caribou hides which they made into buckskin and traded to the coastal Natives. The oil was carried in cedar boxes that usually leaked, so it literally was a grease trail. Now it is called the Alexander Mackenzie Heritage Trail. Mackenzie wrote:

> **"We carried on our backs four bags and a half of pemmican, weighing ninety pounds each, a case with my instruments, a parcel of goods for presents, weighing ninety pounds, and a parcel containing ammunition of the same weight. Each of the Canadians had a burden of about ninety pounds, with a gun and some ammunition. The Indians had about forty-five pounds weight of pemmican to carry, besides their guns, with which they were very dissatisfied, and if they had dared they would have instantly left us. …My own load, and that of Mr. Mackay, consisted of twenty-two pounds of pemmican, some rice, a little sugar, amounting in whole to about seventy pounds each, besides our arms and ammunition. I also had the tube of my telescope swung across my shoulder which was troublesome in addition to my burden."**

Pemmican

(from the Cree language: pimmi = meat and kon = fat)
Pemmican was a staple food for fur traders. It was made from buffalo meat that was sliced thin and then pounded to separate the fibres. The meat was mixed with melted fat and sometimes berries were added. It would keep for the whole winter, which allowed the fur traders and trappers to survive without using valuable time to hunt.

1816
The first bicycle, the "draisine", was invented by Baron von Drais.

1819
Switzerland produced the first factory made chocolate bar.

1822
American surgeon William Beaumont explained digestion.

Mackenzie Rock
The original inscription, done with grease and vermilion dye, wore off and was replaced with this chiselled version in 1926. Mackenzie Rock is the focal point of Sir Alexander Mackenzie Provincial Park.

It was 285 km (180 mi.) from Punchaw Lake to Bella Coola. Going west took them 12 days compared with 15 days for an experienced hiker today. They walked from 5 a.m. to 9 p.m. each day, "A blistering pace," says Mackenzie biographer Derek Hayes. They had to climb a mountain pass to get to the Bella Coola Valley. Mackenzie described it, "The wind rose to a tempest, and the weather was distressing as any I have ever experienced." At Bella Coola they walked into the Nuxalk village that they called Friendly Village. They were welcomed with salmon roe, berries and roasted salmon. On July 17 Mackenzie wrote, "I never enjoyed a more sound and refreshing rest, though I had a board for my bed and a billet (a thick piece of firewood) for my pillow."

Mackenzie was able to borrow two canoes to travel to the sea. Nuxalk Natives went with them and proved to be excellent canoeists. When they reached the Pacific Ocean, they had travelled 1350 km (850 mi.) from Fort Fork in 72 days. Mackenzie set down at the only flat spot available on Dean Channel. He took a longitude reading to establish their location at 10 p.m. on July 22 and then paddled all night to the village of Qomq'ts [Bella Coola]. A man that Mackenzie called "a troublesome fellow" was spreading rumours about being attacked by his party. That misunderstanding was settled and then Mackenzie was able to buy canoes and poles for the return trip.

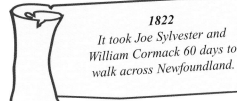

1822
It took Joe Sylvester and William Cormack 60 days to walk across Newfoundland.

1824
The Hudson's Bay Co. established Fort Vancouver which became Victoria in 1843.

1825
The first steam-powered freight and passenger train service began in England.

Two Encounters with the Natives of the Pacific Northwest

Vancouver explored up to Kitimat. He described encounters with the Native people that were usually friendly with much trading for sea otter pelts. Getting information was also important to help with the mapping process. Further north the Natives tended to be more hostile and there was a nasty incident at Traitor's Cove recorded by Vancouver. Near Ketchikan, Alaska, they met a group of Natives in canoes who were quick to steal muskets and anything else they could from the open boats. An old woman was leading the assault and she was able to get hold of the lead line and lash her canoe to their boat. More items were stolen. Vancouver held his musket and spoke to the chief, but the woman encouraged the other Natives to continue to fight. Several members of the crew were wounded with spears. Only the arrival of Vancouver's launch stopped the assault when shots were fired at the Natives. They headed for shore immediately. Happily, the wounds to Vancouver's men were not life-threatening.
Mackenzie describes a similar incident in his journal:" On the way to Mackenzie Rock we met three canoes …with Natives who examined everything we had in our possession with an air of indifference and disdain. One of them made me understand, with an air of insolence, that a large canoe had lately been in the bay, with people in her like me and that one of them whom he called Macuba, had fired on him and his friends and that Bensins had struck him on the back, with the flat part of his sword." Mackenzie guessed that Macuba was Vancouver and Besins was Menzies.

During the trip to Bella Coola, they had lost their dog in one of the villages. On the way back, the Natives told him that the dog had been seen, so they stopped there and looked for him. He was fearful and hungry, so they offered him food and he finally recognized them and returned with the party.

They walked for nine days and reached their food cache and the canoe on August fourth. Mackenzie wanted to carry live salmon across the Continental Divide so that the fish would flourish in the Peace River, but by mid-August his ankles had swollen so that it was difficult for him to walk. He had to abandon that scheme as they were in a hurry to get to Fort Fork. Because they were travelling with the current and the water levels were lower, the trip down the river was relatively easy. They arrived on August 23. Mackenzie wrote:

> "Here my voyages of discovery terminate. Their toils and their dangers, their solicitudes and sufferings have not been exaggerated in my description, on the contrary, in many instances language has failed me in the attempt to describe them. I received, however, the reward of my labours, for they were crowned with success."

Mackenzie travelled back to Fort Chipewyan after having been away for 11 months. He spent the winter there attempting to make a good copy of his journals. He found this to be such a difficult task that years later he hired a ghost writer to complete the work. The inactivity and loneliness and probably the letdown after such a great effort and accomplishment caused him to write the following to his cousin, Roderic, "What a pretty situation I am in this winter. Starving and alone, without the power of doing myself or any body else any Service."

Mackenzie left Athabasca Country for good when he travelled to the partners' meeting in Grand Portage in July 1794. He related the story of his adventures to the businessmen and although the route he had used was not feasible for trade, he expected that an easier one would be found. Simon Fraser found an easier route.

Alexander Mackenzie was knighted in 1802. His journals were published late in 1801. They were reprinted in France, Germany and America. Thomas Jefferson, President of the United States, purchased a copy and gave it to explorers Lewis and Clark. They carried it across the country to the Pacific Ocean in 1805. Mackenzie had good ideas to encourage British expansion, but at the time Britain was not interested in the Pacific Coast of Canada. If Britain had adopted Mackenzie's ideas, the history of the West Coast would have developed quite differently.

In 1812, Mackenzie retired and married at the same time. He and his wife bought an estate on Moray Firth in Scotland and had three children. After only eight years, his health was failing and when he travelled to Edinburgh to see his doctor he was taken ill. Mackenzie died on March 12, 1820 at the age of 58.

> "Sir Alexander Mackenzie had carved himself a place in history, not only as one of the greatest explorers and fur traders in Canada, but also as a pioneer of the development of the Dominion of Canada from the Atlantic to the Pacific. He opened the way for others to follow and gradually, over the years, his dreams for Canada have come true." (JME, grade 7)

Meriwether Lewis and William Clark Expedition
1804 -1806

Thomas Jefferson, President of the United States of America, was interested in the American West. He started to plan an expedition to find a river route across the continent after having read *Voyages from Montréal* by Sir Alexander Mackenzie. Jefferson realized that the Pacific Northwest could become part of the British Empire and he wanted to prevent that. Inspired by the voyages of Captains Cook and Vancouver, Jefferson imagined an expedition of discovery that included science, business and contact with Native peoples.

In 1803, the Louisiana Purchase added a huge portion of the midwestern section of the continent to the U.S.A. Jefferson hired Captain Lewis and Lieutenant Clark to lead the expedition that would introduce American sovereignty to these new lands. In May 1804, the expedition left St. Louis and headed up the Missouri River. The team of 48 men included Lewis, a naturalist, Clark, a mapmaker and negotiator, army soldiers, French boatmen and hunters. Although this part of the river was well known to traders, the voyage was difficult. During the first part of the trip, they were troubled by mosquitoes and gnats and in order to get around the Great Falls on the Missouri River they had to build carts to carry their belongings. They spent the winter at Fort Mandan in North Dakota. In April of 1805,

they set out on the second and harder part of the journey. There were 33 people in the party including Sacajawea, a Native woman, her husband, Toussaint Charbonneau, a French-Canadian interpreter, and their baby son, Baptiste. Sacajawea was a negotiator who was able to help the party trade for horses and supplies when they needed them.

They struggled across the Continental Divide and were troubled by bears in the mountains. Lewis and Clark were surprised that there was no large river on the other side. They trudged through snow and eventually found the Snake River and then the Columbia River, which carried them to the Pacific Ocean in November 1805. They stayed over the winter at Fort Clatsop, near present-day Astoria, Oregon. Before returning to the East, they did some exploring along the Marias River, which they thought might lead into the rich fur trading country that is now Alberta.

Along the way, Native people provided geographical information, transportation, food and shelter. The members of the expedition recorded everything that they found and brought back samples of soil, plants and animals. The information that they reported about furs encouraged fur traders to move further west into the mountains. The party returned to St. Louis via the Missouri River in September 1806.

Lewis and Clark received a hero's welcome. Lewis became governor of the Louisiana Territory and Clark became a Native American agent. This expedition began the tradition of government-sponsored scientific exploration in the United States.

Peace Arch at the British Columbia - Washington Border with "Children of a Common Mother" Part of the Inscription

Natives the Explorers Met

Along the Mackenzie River

Chipewyan means "pointed skins" because their tunics had a dangling tail on the back and sometimes on the front also. They called themselves "Dene" meaning "people". They lived north of the Churchill River all across the North to Great Slave Lake. They hunted in large groups to trap caribou in brush enclosures. When there was open water they drove the caribou into the lakes and rivers and speared them from their canoes.

The fur trade changed their customs dramatically. They had hunted on the Barrens but they started to hunt in the boreal forest too. They learned to use canoes to transport furs more quickly and easily. Formerly they had walked to Hudson Bay!

The Dogrib called themselves "Doné" meaning "the People" and lived north of Great Slave Lake and east of the Mackenzie River. They hunted caribou on the Barrens and moose and hare in the forests.

In British Columbia

In the mid 1700's, the Native population in British Columbia has been estimated by anthropologists at 200,000 to 300,000. The population dropped by 90% to 23,000 by 1929. Diseases such as smallpox, tuberculosis, scarlet fever, influenza, and measles killed the First Nations people because they had no natural immunity to them.

The fur trade had some positive effects. Trading furs for metal carving tools made carving easier and more precise and having metal pots made cooking easier. Native people changed their customs and some moved closer to trading posts.

The Sekani, which means "dwellers on the rocks", lived around the Finlay and Parsnip Rivers in the Rocky Mountains. They hunted moose and caribou.

The Haida had plenty of food so they had time to develop their fine carving. Using European iron tools led to a great increase in productionbecause they could carve more quickly than with tools made of bone, shell or stone.

The Carrier name comes from the custom of widows carrying their dead husbands' ashes in a bag for a year.

Mackenzie described a meeing:

Totem Pole

"Our new acquaintances were people of very pleasing aspect. The hair of the women was tied in large loose knots over the ears and plaited with great neatness from the division of the head so as to be included in the knots. Some of them had adorned their tresses with beads, with very pretty effect. The men were clothed in leather, their hair nicely combed...There was one man amongst them of at least six feet four inches in height, and he had a more prepossessing appearance than any Indian I had met in my journey; he was about 28 years of age and was treated with particular respect by his party."

The Nuxalk (Bella Coola) lived in the Bella Coola Valley area. They hunted, gathered roots and fished for salmon and candlefish, the source of eulachon oil.

Great Rivers of Western Canada

Fraser River

Original Name
- Rio Blanca, named by Spanish Captain Francisco Eliza

Source
- Western slopes of the Rocky Mountains near Jasper.
- Nechako, Chilcotin and Thompson Rivers flow into it.

River Mouth
- Delta 50 km wide at the Strait of Georgia

Length
- 1368 km

Industries
- Forestry
- Agriculture and cattle
- Salmon

Interesting Facts
- Most diverse river system in North America because it crosses many different landscapes
- Fraser Canyon cuts 300-600 m. into bedrock formed during Miocene (2-3million years ago)
- Trans-Canada Highway and 2 railroads are carved into canyon sides
- Fin Donelly has swum the length of the river twice to publicize dangers to the system
- Interior Salish have fished the Fraser River for at least 8000 years
- Water from Mount Robson mixes with salt water in Strait of Georgia in one week

Mackenzie River

Original Name
- Great River or Dehcho by the Dene people
- Disappointment River and Slave River

Source
- Peace River, Athabasca River and Great Slave Lake

River Mouth
- Delta is 80 km across, one of the largest in the world

Length
- 4241 km to the head of the Finlay River
- Longest river in Canada
- Second longest river in North America after the Mississippi River

Industries
- Fur trade
- Oil and gas
- Mining of gold, uranium, tungsten, radium and silver

Interesting Facts
- Relatively warm water flowing to the Arctic Ocean creates a microclimate in which Canada's most northerly forest flourishes
- One of the few unspoiled areas of the world

1826
René Caillie, disguised as an Arab, became the first European to enter Timbuktu and return home alive.

1829
The Welland Canal opened to connect Lakes Erie and Ontario.

1831
The north magnetic pole was discovered by Sir James Ross.

Peace River

Original Name	•Cree and Beaver settled their disputes at Peace Point on its banks
Source	•Williston Lake (created by the damming of the Finlay and Parsnip Rivers)
River Mouth	•At Mackenzie River (its largest tributary)
Length	•1923 km
Industries	•Lumber and pulp from spruce forests •Natural gas and oil •Grains: canola and wheat
Interesting Facts	•Remnants of Fort Fork can be seen at the town of Peace River •Dinosaur tracks have been found along its banks

Athabasca River

Original Names	•Elle and Rivière à la Biche
Source	•Columbia Icefield
River Mouth	•Lake Athabasca
Length	•1231 km
Industries	•Oil sands containing bitumen
Interesting Facts	•Longest and largest river in Alberta and relatively untouched by human engineering •Europeans saw Natives repairing canoes with tar indicating the presence of oil

The Legend of Beaver Face

Once there was a village on the edge of the forest, a scary place where a monster lived so the children were forbidden to go near it. One girl had been born with a split lip so that her teeth showed. Other children called her Beaver Face and teased her cruelly.

While they were playing, the children forgot their fears and wandered close to the forest. Suddenly, a huge creature, very tall and shaggy with black fur and wild eyes, scooped up the children and threw them into a basket on her back. It was Tsonoqua, the Timber Giant. Beaver Face took a small mussel shell knife out of the workbasket that she wore around her waist and cut away the bottom of the basket so that the children could escape. They ran back to the village to get the warriors.

By now the giant had arrived at her house. When she looked in the basket, she was angry because her supper had run away. She was furious with Beaver Face until she noticed her lovely earrings. The giant wanted them so that she would look beautiful. The girl saw that Tsonoqua didn't have pierced ears and that gave her an idea. "If you let me go I will give you my earrings but first I need to make holes in your ears for them." Beaver Face asked the giant to lie down so that she could reach. She drove a spike through one ear into the floor and then through the other ear. With the monster pinned to the ground, she hit her over the head with a stone mallet, killing her.

When the warriors came, they were astounded by what they saw. The dead monster's house was filled with riches such as copper pots, mountain goat and sea otter skins, and woollen blankets. The villagers took these and set fire to the house. They believed the giant was gone but Beaver Face said, "Don't be so sure". A thundering voice rose from the ashes. "Though you burn me I will bite you and drink your blood." The ashes turned into mosquitoes that pester humans to this day.

No one ever called the heroine Beaver Face again; she was called Bright As The Sun.

1832-1888
Louisa May Alcott wrote "Little Women".

1834
Slavery was abolished throughout the British Empire.

1839
Fifty-eight convicted rebels left Québec for exile in Australia.

Simon Fraser
(1776-1862)

Simon Fraser was born near Bennington, Vermont on the family farm. His parents, Simon and Isabella, had seven children when Simon was born. The Frasers were loyal to Britain during the American Revolutionary War. They were disliked because of this and Simon's father was imprisoned. He died when Simon was only three years old. It became necessary for Isabella to sell the farm and move north to Canada. She and her children moved to her eldest son's property near Coteau du Lac, just west of Montréal. Some of her other sons had land near Cornwall, Ontario, where Isabella finally settled.

Simon's uncle, Judge John Fraser, took charge of his schooling in Montréal. Two of his mother's brothers, Peter and Donald Grant, were working in the fur trade. When Simon was 16, he started an apprenticeship as a clerk in the North West Company. Simon's Uncle John knew Simon McTavish, head of the

Simon Fraser

North West Company. They needed strong young men like Simon. He became a partner in 1802 at 25 years of age.

In 1805 at the North West Company meeting in Fort William, the partners instructed Fraser to follow the Peace River, cross the Rocky Mountains and establish trading posts in the interior [British Columbia]. He was also to attempt to follow the Columbia River to its mouth at the Pacific Ocean.

Fraser's first task was to take 20 men along the Peace River to establish Rocky Mountain Portage House at the foot of the Peace River Canyon. He left John Stuart in charge of building and pushed on. Fraser and his crew travelled to the Finlay River and then turned down the Parsnip River. A few days later, they entered the smaller Pack River, which joined Trout Lake. This was later renamed McLeod Lake where Fraser built the first permanent trading post west of the Rocky Mountains called Fort McLeod. Here they met up with friendly Sekani Natives that

Fraser called "Big Men". Fraser left three men at the new fort, then returned to Rocky Mountain House for the winter. Two of the men from Fort McLeod came back to Rocky Mountain House having travelled through the bitterly cold weather. The men could not get along together and eventually the third man returned also.

The next summer Fraser's main objective was to set up a trading post on Stuart Lake in Carrier Indian Territory. John Stuart, the only competent canoe maker, was too busy with other duties to oversee the canoe building, so the three canoes that were built were of poor quality. They were in need of many repairs because they leaked, which slowed the progress of the party. They found three small lakes, the Arctic, Portage and Pacific that led into the Bad River [James Creek]. It was a difficult river to navigate because of fallen trees and rapids, but they persevered. On July 26 they entered Stuart Lake.

Fraser was disappointed when they reached the site of the

43 CANADA

Fraser River
Fleuve Fraser

new fort. Stocks of provisions and trade goods were low and the salmon run was six weeks late. Both the Carrier Natives and Fraser's party were short of food. Even so, they started building the fort which became Fort St. James. Fraser and his crew believed that they were going to explore the Columbia River, but it was actually the Fraser River. The exploration had to be postponed because it would have been foolhardy to begin such a difficult voyage without adequate provisions. Instead, Fraser went further west on the Nechako River to establish Fort Fraser on Fraser Lake. The extra men and supplies that Fraser had requested from the North West Company finally arrived in the fall of 1807. He went east along the Nechako River to where it meets the Fraser River and established Fort George.

By late May of 1808, all was ready for the expedition. There were 24 men in the party including the voyageurs LaChapelle, Baptiste, D'Alaire, LaCerte, Bourboné, Gagier, and LaGarde. There were also two Natives, one of whom

Fraser called "Our Little Fellow." Fraser said the river was treacherous with "tremendous gulphs and whirlpools...ready every moment to swallow a Canoe with all its contents and the people on board." On June 5 he wrote:

> *The current throughout the day ran with amazing velocity and on this and the last course our situation was really dangerous, being constantly between steep and high banks where there was no possibility of stopping the canoe, and even if it could be stopped, there would be no such thing as going up the hills, so that had we suddenly come upon a cascade or bad Rapid, not to mention falls, it is more than likely that all of us would have perished..."*

Fraser Canyon

Fraser described the surrounding land as fine country abounding with plenty of animals such as moose, red deer, caribou, beaver and horses that the Natives used.

Many of their days were similar. They embarked by 5 a.m. with some of the men taking the canoes down the river with the provisions and the others walking through the rough country carrying the guns, ammunition and personal belongings. They often lost time because they had to stop and mend their shoes. Their feet developed blisters and were sore from the difficult terrain. A pair of shoes hardly lasted a day and their feet became full of thorns. Often the weather was very hot or rainy and nights were cold when they were in the mountains. Every day they met Natives who lived along the river or came from inland because they were curious to see the Europeans. They met Natives from the Atnah, Thompson, Interior Salish, Chilcotin and Coastal Salish tribes who were welcoming and fed them with salmon, berries, oils and roots. The Natives had European or Russian goods such as copper teakettles, brass camp kettles and guns. Fraser described their stay with the Thompson Natives:

1841-1919
Sir Wilfrid Laurier was Canada's seventh and first francophone prime minister.

1842
The first operation using an anesthetic was performed in Georgia.

1847-1848
More than 9000 Irish immigrants died of typhus en route to Canada.

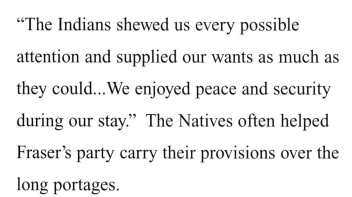

"The Indians shewed us every possible attention and supplied our wants as much as they could...We enjoyed peace and security during our stay." The Natives often helped Fraser's party carry their provisions over the long portages.

The most dangerous part of the expedition occurred at Hell's Gate. Fraser described it in his journal:

June 26 *"As for the road by land we scarcely could make our way in some parts even with our guns. I have been for a long period among the Rocky Mountains, but have never seen anything equal to this country, for I cannot find words to describe our situation at times. We had to pass where no human being should venture."*

July 10 *"Set out early. Kept the left side of the river accompanied by several Indians who shewed us the way. The road was inconceivably bad. We had to pass many difficult rocks, defiles and precipices, through which there was a kind of beaten path used by the natives, and made passable by means of scaffolds, bridges and ladders so peculiarly constructed, that it required no small degree of necessity, dexterity and courage in strangers to undertake a passage through such intricacies of apparent danger as we had to encounter on this occasion. For instance we had to ascend precipices by means of ladders composed of two long poles placed upright and parallel with sticks crossways tied with twigs.... Add to this that the ladders were often so slack that the smallest breeze put them on motion - swinging them against the rocks - while the steps were so narrow and irregular leading from scaffold to scaffold, that they could scarcely be traced by the feet without the greatest care and circumspection;*

but the most perilous was, when another rock projected over the one you were leaving. The Indians deserve our thanks for their able assistance through these alarming situations.

The descents were still worse. In these places we were under necessity of trusting all our things to the Indians, even our guns were handed from one to another. Yet they thought nothing of these difficulties, but went up and down these wild places with the same agility as sailors do on board of a ship."

Fraser Shooting the Rapids
"The struggle which the men on this trial experienced between the whirlpools and rocks almost exhausted their strength; the canoes were in perpetual danger of sinking or being broken into pieces. It was a desperate undertaking."
(Fraser's Journal, June 4, 1808)

1849
Levi Strauss began the manufacture of blue jeans.

1858
The first pencil with an attached eraser was patented in Philadelphia.

1862
Modern soccer rules were drafted by Englishman J.C.Thring.

Fraser and his men borrowed canoes from the Natives to complete their expedition to the Pacific Ocean. They saw seals and huge cedar trees. Mosquitoes attacked them in clouds and they had very little to eat. Although the Natives fed them well in their villages, they were not given food to take with them. Following the North Arm of the Fraser River, they came within sight of the Strait of Georgia where they met up with hostile Natives. At one time, the Natives tried to surround them in their canoes, but Fraser and his men threatened them with their guns and the Natives retreated.

At the Pacific Ocean, Fraser took latitude readings and finally realized that they had not found the Columbia River at all. He knew from previous explorers' charts that it was south of their present position.

Although at times they were pursued by angry Natives and had to paddle all night to escape, there were also friendly Natives along the way who brought them fish. The men wanted to abandon the river and walk because the expedition had been so difficult and they still had to go back through Hell's Gate.

Fraser was successful in persuading them to continue as planned. Natives helped them all along the way on their return journey.

When they arrived above Hell's Gate, they found their canoes intact and later local people returned hats and shoes that they had lost in the rapids. Natives had watched their caches of provisions to keep the wild animals away so that they would have food for the return trip. "Our Little Fellow" left the expedition when they met the Atnahs again. He had stayed with them throughout the journey and often went on ahead to help with guiding and interpreting for them. The party returned to Fort George on August 6, 1808.

Fraser continued to work for the North West Company for ten years but in 1818 he was happy to retire to St. Andrews near Cornwall.

FRASER/RETURNING FROM THE PACIFIC/RETOUR DU PACIFIQUE

He farmed, operated two mills and lived a quiet family life with his wife, Catherine Macdonell and their eight children. During the Rebellion of 1837, Fraser was a Captain in the Stormont Militia. He had a bad fall while on duty, that severely injured his knee, so that walking was difficult for him for the rest of his life.

Fraser spent many hours of his retirement reading, thereby making up for his lack of formal education as a young man. He was well informed and extremely interested in Canadian politics.

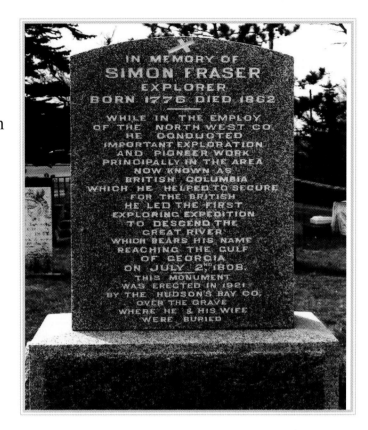

Simon Fraser died on August 11, 1862 at 86 years of age. Surprisingly, his wife died the very next day even before she had been told of Fraser's death. They are buried in this grave in St. Andrews.

Conclusion

Cook, Vancouver, Mackenzie and Fraser were all remarkable explorers, instrumental in opening Canada to trade and settlement.

Captain James Cook has been described as perhaps the most important figure in the history of maritime exploration. He was certainly that in Canadian maritime history because he charted the St. Lawrence River at Québec, the entire Newfoundland coast and the West Coast of Canada. He was a man of rare talent with a noble bearing who commanded respect because of his fairness and his ability.

Captain George Vancouver completed the huge task of charting 15,000 km (9000 miles) of the Pacific Northwest Coast in open boats with the loss of only two men. He ratified the Nootka Convention and so completed all the tasks assigned to him on his voyage.

Sir Alexander Mackenzie's expeditions were commercially motivated but the explorer in him wanted to find out where the rivers went and thus fill in some spaces on the map of Canada. Biographer Derek Hayes says, "He had a real

role to play in linking what is today the western part of the country to Canada."

Simon Fraser set up trading posts in British Columbia and explored a most difficult river. Max Finkelstein, the man who followed Mackenzie's route by canoe says, "This is a river with a mean reputation, well deserved. It runs fast, continuously fast. There are no pools below the rapids, just the relentless current...The Fraser does not flow in the sense of a normal river. It seethes, it fumes, it roars."

Finkelstein sums up his experience of the Canadian wilderness: "Alexander Mackenzie's route embodies a wellspring of Canadian heritage and history. To a large extent, the route defines Canada and what being Canadian means... The land and water have sung and danced and wept with me. In the wild places, in the ancient places, in the quiet places, the land really does sing. You can hear it if you stop and listen."

Glossary

Archipelago:	a group of islands
Arduous :	hard to achieve or overcome
Aristocrats:	people of noble birth usually wealthy and having high social status
Cache:	a hiding place, often used to store food, supplies, etc.
Condescend:	behave as if one is on equal terms but maintaining an attitude of superiority
Continental Divide:	the boundary between separate drainage basins on a continent
Credentials:	evidence of one's achievements and trustworthiness
Despot:	an absolute ruler, tyrant or oppressor
Disposition:	one's temperament or character, especially as shown in dealings with others
Endeavour:	an earnest or strenuous attempt to attain a goal
Fife:	a kind of small flute used with a drum in military music
Flora and fauna:	the plants and animals in a region
Fluctuated:	rose or fell or changed irregularly
Gentry:	people of high social standing
Hygiene:	practice of maintaining good health by cleanliness
Perpendicular:	vertical, straight up
Protozoans:	any one-celled or microscopic organism of the subkingdom Protozoa
Protuberant:	bulging
Ratify:	to confirm or accept an agreement by signature
Synchronize:	to cause to occur at the same time
Tributaries:	all the streams and small rivers that feed into a larger river
Vertebrate:	any animal having a spinal column

Dafoe, Daniel. ROBINSON CRUSOE. New York City: Atheneum Books for Young Readers, 1983. Written in 1713, this fictional tale of a shipwrecked sailor is based on the story of Alexander Selkirk.

Garfield, Leon. THE APPRENTICES. New York City: Mammoth, 1976 and 2002. A dozen linked stories of skulduggery and human relations reveal the lives of adolescents in 18th century London.

Gaetz, Dayle. THE GOLDEN ROSE. Vancouver: Pacific Educational Press, 1996. A voyage across the Atlantic in the 1860's brings Katherine to a difficult new life near the Fraser River.

Hesse, Karen. STOWAWAY. New York City: Aladdin Paperbacks, 2000. Cook's remarkable voyage of 1768 is re-created through the eyes of Nicholas Young, a real-life boy who stowed away on *Endeavour*.

Hobbs, Will. GHOST CANOE. New York City: Avon Books, 1997. Set in 1874, this rivetting mystery involves the Northwest Pacific, a ghostly canoe, a skeleton, ancient treasure and murder.

Klinck, George. DOWN TO THE SEA. Richmond Hill, ON: Simon& Schuster, 1967. Here is an original adventure story based on the explorations of Simon Fraser.

Lawrence, Iain. THE BUCCANEERS. New York City: Delacorte Press, 2001. In the third title in the High Seas Trilogy it is 1803 and all the buccaneers are long gone but Bartholomew is desperate to locate a fabled lost treasure.

Lawson, Julie. A RIBBON OF SHINING STEEL. Markham, ON: Scholastic Canada, 2002. Kate, who lives in Yale, BC in 1882, writes in her diary, "Hell's Gate is not a blasphemy even though it contains the "H" word. It is a real place on the Canyon so I can say it."

Manson, Ainslie. A DOG CAME TOO. Toronto: Groundwood, 1992. For younger readers, this illustrated book tells the true story of the dog that crossed to the Pacific with Mackenzie.

Walsh, Ann (editor). BEGINNINGS: STORIES OF CANADA'S PAST. Vancouver: Ronsdale Press, 2001. This short story collection includes "First Encounter", an imagined account of the first contact between Native people in central BC and Simon Fraser.

Wilson, Eric. SPIRIT IN THE RAINFOREST. Toronto: Collins, 1984. The Austens survive a hair-raising Pacific storm and investigate the wailing cry of a girl in the wilds of Vancouver Island.

Wilson, Eric. THE EMILY CARR MYSTERY. Toronto: Harper Collins, 2001. Teen sleuth Liz Austen is caught up in some nasty business including the theft of an Emily Carr painting while visiting in Victoria.

Beyer, Don E. THE TOTEM POLE INDIANS OF THE NORTHWEST. Danbury, CT: Franklin Watts, 1989.

Bial, Raymond. THE HAIDA. New York City: Benchmark Books, 2001.

Campbell. Marjorie Wilkins. THE SAVAGE RIVER: SEVENTY-ONE DAYS WITH SIMON FRASER. Toronto: Macmillan, 1968 & 2002.

Cass, James. OYAI: THE SALMON FISHERMAN AND THE WOODWORKER. Toronto: Heath Canada, 1983.

Garrod, Stan. VOYAGES OF DISCOVERY. Don Mills, ON: Fitzhenry & Whiteside, 1987.

Harris, Christie. ONCE MORE UPON A TOTEM. Toronto: McClelland & Stewart, 1973.

Haig-Brown, Roderick. CAPTAIN OF THE DISCOVERY: THE STORY OF CAPTAIN GEORGE VANCOUVER. Toronto: Macmillan, 1974.

Langley, Andrew. EXPLORING THE PACIFIC: THE EXPEDITIONS OF CAPTAIN COOK. New York City: Chelsea Juniors, 1994.

Liptak, Karen. THE FIRST AMERICANS: INDIANS OF THE PACIFIC NORTHWEST. New York City: Facts on File, 1991.

Livesey, Robert and A.G. Smith. THE FUR TRADERS. Toronto: Stoddart, 1989.

Livesey, Robert and A.G. Smith. NATIVE PEOPLES. Toronto: Stoddart, 1993.

McConkey, Lois. SEA AND CEDAR: HOW THE NORTH WEST COAST INDIANS LIVED. Vancouver: J.J. Douglas Ltd., 1973.

Manson, Ainslie. SIMON FRASER. Toronto: Grolier, 1991.

Mercredi, Morningstar. FORT CHIPEWYAN HOMECOMING: A JOURNEY TO NATIVE CANADA. Markham, ON: Fitzhenry & Whiteside, 1998.

Morriss, Roger. CAPTAIN COOK AND HIS EXPLORATION OF THE PACIFIC. Hauppauge, NJ: Barron's, 1998.

Santor, Donald. DISCOVERY AND EXPLORATION: A CANADIAN ADVENTURE. Scarborough, ON: Prentice-Hall, 1985.

Shemmie, Bonnie. HOUSES OF WOOD. Montreal: Tundra. 1992.

Shields, Charles J. JAMES COOK AND THE EXPLORATION OF THE PACIFIC. Philadelphia: Chelsea House, 2002.

Smith, James K. ALEXANDER MACKENZIE. Don Mills, ON: Fitzhenry & Whiteside, 1976.

Syme, Ronald. VANCOUVER: EXPLORER OF THE PACIFIC COAST. New York City: Morrow, 1970.

Waterlow, Julia. THE EXPLORER THROUGH HISTORY. Hove, U.K.: Wayland, 1994.

White, Ellen. KWULASULWUT: STORIES FROM THE COAST SALISH. Penticton: Theytus Books, 1992.

Wilson, Keith. FUR TRADE IN CANADA. Toronto: Grolier, 1980.

Xydes, Georgia. ALEXANDER MACKENZIE AND THE EXPLORERS OF CANADA. New York City: Chelsea House, 1992.

Zuehlke, Mark. FUN B.C. FACTS FOR KIDS. Vancouver: Whitecap Books, 1996.

Places to Visit

BRITISH COLUMBIA

Alexander Mackenzie Heritage Trail
The 347 km trail from Quesnel to Dean Channel would require 18 to 24 days to complete. You can hike for a few hours or a day.

Fort Langley National Historic Site
Langley, 604-888-4424
www.parkscanada.pch.gc.ca
Established on the Fraser River 19 years after Fraser's voyage, the Crown Colony of B.C. was inaugurated here in 1858. The first storehouse still stands. (p. 33)

Fort St. James National Historic Site
Fort St. James, 250-996-7191
www.parkscanada.gc.ca/james
This fully restored Hudson's Bay Company post (founded by Stuart and Fraser) commemorates the fur trade from 1806 to 1952.

Fraser-Fort George Regional Museum
Prince George, 250-562-1612
www.theexplorationplace.com
The site of the fort that Fraser founded in 1807 now includes exhibits on Native peoples, transportation and lumber.

Friendly Cove, near Gold River
Visit the Catholic Church to see the window commemorating Vancouver's and Quadra's historic meeting (p. 28), and take a cruise to explore the Cove and Nootka Sound.

Gwaii Haanas National Park Reserve and Haida Heritage Site,
Queen Charlotte, 250-559-8818
http://parkscan.harbour.com/gwaii
Those visiting this challenging north coast environment must be experienced in wilderness and marine travel.

Hell's Gate Airtram, near Boston Bar
604-867-9277. www.hellsgateairtram.com
Descend 153 m across the narrowest part of the Fraser Canyon and imagine canoeing this thundering waterway in 1808.

'Ksan Historical Village and Museum
The Hazeltons, 877-842-5518
www.ksan.org. This replicated village illustrates many aspects of the ancient Gitxsan culture. Watch carvers, hear legends and enjoy salmon prepared the old way.

Kwakwaka'wakw Museum and Cultural Centre, Cape Mudge
Quadra Island, 250-285-3733
Fascinating, ancient petroglyphs and an exceptional collection of Native artifacts can be seen here.

Maritime Museum of B.C., Victoria
250-385-4222. www.mmbc.bc.ca
Explore B.C.'s maritime heritage via displays of ship models, figureheads, bells, uniforms, and the "Tillicum", a dugout canoe modified into a schooner which sailed from Victoria to England 100 years ago.

Places to Visit

BRITISH COLUMBIA

Museum of Anthropology, U.B.C.
Vancouver, 604-822-5087
www.moa.ubc.ca. See spectacular
sculptures, ceramics, totem poles,
houses, etc., all representative of the
Native peoples of B.C.

Petroglyph Provincial Park, Nanaimo
Marvel at prehistoric sandstone carvings
of humans, wolves, birds and lizards.

Quw'utsun' Cultural Centre, Duncan
877-746-8119. www.quwutsun.ca
Experience aboriginal life, especially
cuisine and dance and see how baskets
and totems are created.

Royal B.C. Museum, Victoria
888-447-7977
www.royalbcmuseum.bc.ca
Journey back in time for an in-depth
look at 12,000 years of natural and
human history. Don't miss a simulated
voyage with Vancouver on *Discovery*.

Thunderbird Park, Victoria
Watch carvers at work making cedar
dugout canoes and totems and explore
a replica of a 19th century Native house.

Vancouver Maritime Museum, Vancouver
604-666-3201. www.vmm.bc.ca
The Children's Maritime Discovery
Centre features activities to introduce
youngsters to ships and pirates. Next door
sits the "St. Roch", the first vessel to
navigate the Northwest Passage from
west to east.

UNITED KINGDOM

British Empire & Commonwealth Museum
Bristol, England
www.empiremuseum.co.uk
Beginning with Cabot's landfall in Nfld.,
16 galleries highlight many aspects of the
Empire including trade, slavery, war and
problems of industrial development.

Captain Cook Memorial Museum
Whitby, England
www.cookmuseumwhitby.co.uk
This museum, housed in the building
where Cook lived as an apprentice
seaman, pays tribute to the great
navigator and exhibits an accurate
model of *Resolution*.

Websites and Picture Credits

The Alexander Mackenzie Voyageur Route
www.amvr.org
Learn more about the route proclaimed by Canada, 6 provinces and one territory as a
"thread that binds the nation".

Canadian Heritage Rivers System
www.chrs.ca
The System encourages Canadians to protect, enjoy and appreciate our rivers. Increase your knowledge of the
Fraser and many others.

Captain Cook Society
www.captaincooksociety.com
This site provides the searcher with links to over 300 other sites.

Encyclopedia of B.C.
www.knowbc.com
You will find additional background information and a sampling of what is available in the print and
CD-ROM editions of the encyclopedia.

Endeavour Replica
www.barkendeavour.com.au
The *Endeavour* replica has sailed around the world and the ship and the web site are sources of information
about Cook and 18th century navigation. (p. 15)

Exploration, The Fur Trade and Hudson's Bay Company
www.canadiana.org/hbc/
Become more familiar with the many adventurers connected with the fur trade, including Mackenzie, and the
Natives who were their teachers and friends.

Historica Foundation
www.histori.ca
The Heritage Minutes and all facets of The Canadian Encyclopedia are at your fingertips at this all-inclusive
web site.

Picture Credits

Bibliography

Cutter, Donald C. MALASPINA AND GALIANO: SPANISH VOYAGES TO THE NORTHWEST COAST, 1791 AND 1792. Vancouver: Douglas & McIntyre, 1991.

Edwards, Philip (editor). THE JOURNALS OF CAPTAIN COOK. London: Penguin, 1999.

Ferguson, Will. CANADIAN HISTORY FOR DUMMIES. Toronto: CDG Books, 2000.

Finkelstein, Max. CANOEING A CONTINENT: ON THE TRAIL OF ALEXANDER MACKENZIE. Toronto: Natural Heritage, 2002.

Fisher, Robin. CONTACT AND CONFLICT: INDIAN -EUROPEAN RELATIONS IN BRITISH COLUMBIA, 1774-1890. Vancouver: UBC Press, 1992.

Francis, Daniel (editor). THE ENCYCLOPEDIA OF BRITISH COLUMBIA. Madeira Park, BC: Harbour Publishing, 2000.

Gillespie, Brenda Guild. ON STORMY SEAS: THE TRIUMPHS AND TORMENTS OF CAPTAIN GEORGE VANCOUVER. Victoria: Horsdal & Schubart, 1992.

Glavin, Terry. THE LAST GREAT SEA: A VOYAGE THROUGH THE HUMAN AND NATURAL HISTORY OF THE NORTH PACIFIC OCEAN. Vancouver: Greystone Books, 2000.

Gough, Barry. FIRST ACROSS THE CONTINENT: SIR ALEXANDER MACKENZIE. Toronto: McClelland & Stewart, 1997.

Gough, Barry. THE NORTHWEST COAST: BRITISH NAVIGATION, TRADE AND DISCOVERIES TO 1812. Vancouver: UBC Press, 1992.

Granatstein, J.L. and Norman Hillmer. FIRST DRAFTS: EYEWITNESS ACCOUNTS FROM CANADA'S PAST. Toronto: Thomas Allen, 2002.

Griffin-Short, Rita. "The Transit of Venus." The Beaver, April/May, 2003.

Harding, Les. THE JOURNEYS OF REMARKABLE WOMEN. Waterloo: Escart Press, 1994.

Hayes, Derek. FIRST CROSSING: ALEXANDER MACKENZIE, HIS EXPEDITION ACROSS NORTH AMERICA AND THE OPENING OF THE CONTINENT. Vancouver: Douglas & McIntyre, 2001.

Hayes, Derek. HISTORICAL ATLAS OF THE NORTH PACIFIC OCEAN. Vancouver: Douglas & McIntyre, 2001.

Horowitz, Tony. BLUE LATITUDES: BOLDLY GOING WHERE CAPTAIN COOK HAS GONE BEFORE. New York City: Henry Holt, 2002.

Hough, Richard. CAPTAIN JAMES COOK: A BIOGRAPHY. New York City: W.W. Norton, 1994.

King, J.C.H. FIRST PEOPLES FIRST CONTACTS: NATIVE PEOPLES OF NORTH AMERICA. Cambridge, MA: Harvard University Press, 1999.

Lamb, W. Kaye (editor). THE JOURNALS AND LETTERS OF SIR ALEXANDER MACKENZIE. Toronto: Macmillan, 1970.

Lamb, W.Kaye (editor). THE LETTERS AND JOURNALS OF SIMON FRASER, 1806-1808. Toronto: Macmillan, 1960.

Lamb, W. Kaye (editor). A VOYAGE OF DISCOVERY TO THE NORTH PACIFIC OCEAN AND ROUND THE WORLD, 1791-1795. London: Hakluyt Society, 1984.

Muckle, Robert J. THE FIRST NATIONS OF BRITISH COLUMBIA: AN ANTHROPOLOGICAL SURVEY. Vancouver: UBC Press, 1998.

Normandin, Christine (editor). ECHOES OF THE ELDERS: THE STORIES AND PAINTINGS OF CHIEF LELOOSKA. New York City: D K Publishing, 1997.

Raban, Jonathan. PASSAGE TO JUNEAU: A SEA AND ITS MEANING. New York City: Pantheon Books, 1999.

Suthren, Victor. TO GO UPON DISCOVERY: JAMES COOK AND CANADA, FROM 1758-1779. Toronto: Dundurn Press, 2000.

Synge, M.B. A BOOK OF DISCOVERY. London, U.K.: Nelson, 1967.

Thomson, Don W. MEN AND MERIDIANS Vol. I. Ottawa: Queen's Printer, 1975.

Villiers, Alan. "The Man Who Mapped the Pacific." National Geographic, September 1971.

Index

Index